I Told You I Was Sick

I Told You I Was Sick

A Grave book of Curious Epitaphs

NIGEL REES

Weidenfeld & Nicolson
Wellington House, 125 Strand, London WC2R 0BB

First published in Great Britain in 2005

10 9 8 7 6 5 4 3 2 1

A CIP catalogue record for this book is available from the
British Library.

ISBN 0 304 36803 2

Design by www.carrstudio.co.uk

Printed and bound in Great Britain by Clays Ltd, St Ives plc

www.orionbooks.co.uk

PREFACE

I have been tempted to apply the well-worn publishing phrase 'comic and curious' to this collection of epitaphs. But few, if any, are likely to provoke thigh-slapping merriment in the reader and seeking laughter in any graveyard seems a little out of keeping.

So I have settled on the word 'curious' and *I Told You I Was Sick* certainly lives up to that word. The epitaphs I have gathered range from the consciously jokey (such as the one in the title), through the unintentionally bizarre, to the straightforwardly interesting attempt to put something a little different on a gravestone. They are all curious, if only in the sense that they are quirky, off-beat, somehow different or just plain odd – in the capriciousness with which they tell you so little about the dear departed or, in one or two cases, tell you so much more than you need to know.

As such, this book continues the centuries-old custom of collecting 'interesting' epitaphs, but I would hope with rather more than the usual level of accuracy in transcription, details of location and of context.

There is an honourable tradition of epitaph collections – the London Library has shelves full of them – from Stow (1598), Camden (1610) and Weever (1631) to the rather less honourable rash of little books full of 'comic and curious' epitaphs published in the second half of the 20th century. These last seem mainly to recycle earlier books and perpetuate their mistakes.

The most curious thing about comic and quirky epitaphs, however, is that they should ever have existed at all, but exist they undoubtedly have done, for centuries (see, for example, that on Stephen Rumbold), though it is often impossible to find the originals now.

And that, of course, is one of the problems with gravestones and memorials. If they are in the open air, they are subject to acid rain and other forms of wear and tear, and it is unusual for them to survive from before, say, 1800, in a legible form. Even indoors (it is a smidgen discomforting to discover), Shakespeare's memorable epitaph at Stratford was so decayed a century after his death that it had to be re-cut.

Where only part of the total wording on a grave or memorial is given in *I Told You I Was Sick*, omissions are indicated by dots, thus ... An asterisk* indicates that the text has been checked by me against the original grave or memorial, or against a photograph.

What strikes me, looking at old epitaph books, is how careless so many of the transcriptions are. I have made a special effort to reproduce the lay-out and capitalization of the original epitaphs, where possible, though not the various sizes and styles of lettering. Where I am sure of the original spelling, I have retained it, while mostly turning 'ye' into 'the', 'yt' into 'that', and so on. Where a 'U' has been cut as a 'V', this has not usually been retained. I make no claims for accurate reproduction of the original punctuation which may now be quite impossible to decipher.

It has, for me, been an immensely enjoyable experience, 'grubbing in churchyards' as John Aubrey put it, but if I might make a plea, it would be that those who look after graveyards could do visitors an immense service by signposting the way to significant graves.

I give thanks to the many people who have drawn curious and interesting epitaphs to my attention, especially when they have also provided me with ancillary information. These include: Su Barkla, Ralf Bates, Natasha Coombs, Joe Kralich, Clarissa Palmer, Chris Partridge, Brian Robinson, Peter Soper, Christopher W. Tarry, Jim Trainor, David Eddershaw, as well as those mentioned in the text.

On the whole, I have tried to confine my selection to those epitaphs that may actually have appeared on gravestones at some time or other. This means that I have decided not to include all those suggested epitaphs for people who might not even have been dead at the time of composition. I am thinking of lines like Dryden's 'Epitaph intended for his wife':

9

Here lies my wife: here let her lie!
Now she's at rest, and so am I.

Or Michael Caine's reply to the question much posed to celebrities over the years, 'What would you like your epitaph to be?':

Been There, Done That.

I have also tried to limit myself to those epitaphs of which I have some indication that they did once exist somewhere. I am told that a blues singer in the Deep South really did have the epitaph:

Didn't wake up this morning ...

– but unfortunately I don't have a shred of evidence for it ...

As to the suggestion that a man called Thomas Longbottom, who died young, was buried under the tag:

Ars longa, vita brevis

I think we are probably looking at an old *Punch* joke here (though I can't give you chapter and verse). It was contributed to BBC Radio *Quote...Unquote* (17 May 1978) by Harry Miller of Prestwich, Manchester. In the same edition, Richard Stilgoe suggested rather that *Punch* in its early days had reproduced the death announcement of a man called 'Longbottom' and put over it the headline 'Vita brevis'

My last word must be: why not go and out do a spot of 'grubbing about in churchyards' yourself? In search of epitaphs, you will make many discoveries, both touching and amusing. Meanwhile, for the chair-bound, I hope this little book will indeed add up to a 'nice derangement of epitaphs', as Mrs Malaprop so splendidly described it in Sheridan's *The Rivals* (1775).

Let the grubbing begin.

NIGEL REES
2005

The Epitaphs

In his *Collections and Recollections* (1898), G.W.E. Russell referred to this as 'the best-known of all epitaphs' but there are grave doubts as to whether what is undoubtedly the most delightful of epitaphs ever existed anywhere at all.

Its first recorded appearance is in *Notes & Queries*, 8:274 (1853) where it is described as being 'from the churchyard of Pewsey, Wiltshire', and it was also featured in one of the earliest numbers of Charles Dickens's magazine *Household Words* (published from 1850 onwards). It was again referred to in *Punch* (29 January 1870) as a 'famous Irish epitaph' (albeit with 'affable' in place of 'passionate', and 'niece' in place of 'first cousin'). Later collections of epitaphs place it in 'Pewsey, Bedfordshire' (which does not exist) (1876); in Dorset (1901); in Devon (1910), and in Bridgewater Cemetery, Somerset (1973). A 1969 collection had this from Bandon in Ireland:

> Sacred to the memory of Mrs Maria Boyle
> Who was a good wife, a devoted Mother
> And a kind and charitable neighbour.
> She painted in water colours,
> And was the first cousin to the Earl of Cork,
> And of such is the Kingdom of Heaven.

But one doubts whether this ever existed either, and it is certainly no longer to be seen. The surname O'Looney does not occur in the *Dictionary of National Biography* nor in *Debrett*, though there were 56 people with the name on British electoral rolls in 2002.

Here lies the body of
LADY O'LOONEY
Great niece of BURKE
Commonly called the Sublime
She was Bland, Passionate
and deeply Religious, also
she painted in water colours
and sent several pictures
to the Exhibition
She was first Cousin to
LADY JONES
and of such is the
Kingdom of Heaven.

On a ‘ledger stone’ in the chancel, immediately before the altar steps, of the church of St Andrew, Bramfield, Suffolk. The epitaph is less bad-tempered, however, than that of Bridgett Applewhaite's husband, Arthur, whose gravestone is immediately to the right of hers. It appears that Arthur died intestate to spite her (she having inherited her father's property) and quite a proportion of that 'easy widowhood' was taken up with lawsuits to recover her patrimony from Arthur's brother. This is expressed in an *inscription, possibly contrived by Bridgett herself, which reads, in part:

'Here lies the Body of ARTHUR APPLEWHAITE...[who died, aged 39, in 1733] ... He Married BRIDGETT the Eldest Daughter, and at length, Sole Heiress of LAMBERT NELSON late of this Parish Gent, By Whom he had no Issue. And to whom (Having by his Father's Instigation made no will) He left no legacy, But a Chancery-Suit with his Eldest Brother For her own Paternal Estates In this Town, and Blyford.'

The 'M S' at the top of the slab is one of a number of common abbreviations for Latin phrases used on gravestones – it is short for *Memoriae Sacrum*, meaning 'sacred to the

M S

Between the Remains of her Brother EDWARD,
And of her Husband ARTHUR
Here lies the Body of BRIDGETT APPLEWHAITE
Once BRIDGETT NELSON.
After the Fatigues of a Married Life,
Born by her with Incredible Patience,
For four years and three Quarters, bating three Weeks;
And after the Enjoiment of the Glorious Freedom
Of an Early and Unblemisht Widowhood,
For four Years and Upwards,
She Resolved to run the Risk of a Second Marriage-Bed
But DEATH forbad the Banns —-
And having with an Apoplectick Dart,
(The same Instrument, with which he had Formerly
Dispatch't her Mother,)
Touch't the most Vital part of her Brain;
She must have fallen Directly to the Ground,
(as one Thunder-strook,)
If she had not been Catch't and Supported
by her Intended Husband,
Of which Invisible Bruise,
After a Struggle for above Sixty Hours
With that Grand Enemy to Life,
(But the Certain and Mercifull Friend to Helpless Old Age,)
In Terrible Convulsions Plaintive Groans, or Stupefying
Sleep,
Without Recovery of her Speech, or Senses,
She Dyed, on the 12th Day of Sept: in ye Year
(of our Lord 1737
(and
(of her own Age 44.

Behold! I Come, as a Theif. Rev. 16th Ch. 15th V.

But Oh! Thou source of Pious Cares
Strict Iudge without Regard
Grant, tho' we Go hence Unawares,
We Go not Unprepar'd.

AMEN

17

Chris Partridge of Fishbourne told me he had seen this epitaph for himself in the old churchyard of Stockbridge, Hampshire. It commemorates John Bucket, landlord of the Kings Head there in the 18th century.

And is, alas, poor Bucket gone?
Farewell, convivial honest John.
Oft at the well by fatal stroke
Buckets like Pitchers must be broke.
In this same motley shifting scene
How various have thy fortunes been
Now lifted high, now sinking low,
Today thy brim would overflow,
Thy bounty then would all supply
To fill and drink and leave thee dry.
Tomorrow sunk as in a well
Content unseen with Truth to dwell:
But high, or low, or wet or dry,
No rotten stave could malice spy.
Then rise, immortal Bucket, rise,
And claim thy station in the skies.

By far the most visited grave in Père-Lachaise Cemetery, Paris, these days, is that of the American-born pop singer, Jim Morrison of The Doors. He died in an alcoholic daze at the age of 27 in 1971. His grave has become a shrine to which fans repair and leave rather curious tributes (joints, candles, poems). The original effigy became worn away, was stolen and then, in 1991, replaced by a breezeblock with a brass plaque on it, bearing the words shown opposite.

But what does the Greek mean? Something like 'In accordance with his own genius' (or 'he did it *his* way') has been suggested. But how strange to put an epitaph on a grave that is incomprehensible to most people who visit it ...

JAMES DOUGLAS MORRISON
1945-1971

ΚΑΤΑ ΤΟΝ ΔΑΙΜΟΝΑ ΕΑΥΤΟΥ

'Here lies Arthur, the once and future king' – that is what, in *Le Morte d'Arthur* (about 1450), Sir Thomas Malory says was written on the tombstone of the legendary King Arthur. On the other hand, if a King Arthur did exist (in the 6th century AD, if at all), there is a notice in the ruins of Glastonbury Abbey, Somerset, that claims to mark the site of his tomb. It states:

'In the year 1191, the bodies of King Arthur and Queen Guinevere were said to have been found on the south side of the Lady Chapel. On 19th April 1278, their remains were removed in the presence of King Edward I and Queen Eleanor to a black marble tomb on this site. This tomb survived until the dissolution of the abbey in 1539.'

Hic jacet Arthurus,
rex quondam
rexque futurus.

From Mitcham Cemetery, Mitcham, London, and quoted in
Hugh Meller, *London Cemeteries* (1981):

Mary, Sarah and Eliza Atwood...who were poisoned by eating funguous vegetables mistaken for champignons on the 11th day of October 1808 and died at the ages of 14, 7 and 5 years within a few hours of each other in excruciating circumstances. The Father, Mother and now, alas, an only child, partakers of the same meal, have survived with debilitated constitutions and to lament so dreadful a calumny. This monument is erected to perpetuate the fatal events as an awful caution to others, let it be too a solemn a warning that in our most grateful enjoyments even in our necessary food may lurk deadly poison ...

From the *slab on the grave in the North Aisle of the
nave of Winchester Cathedral. The novelist Jane Austen
(1775–1817) died at Winchester, having completed *Emma*
the previous year; *Northanger Abbey* and *Persuasion* were
published posthumously in 1818. The inscription makes no
direct mention of her works, but there is a brass *plaque
on the wall beside her grave that does. It states:

'Jane Austen known to many by her writings, endeared
to her family by the buried charms of her Character, and
ennobled by Christian Faith and Piety, was born at ...'

The plaque also quotes Proverbs 31:26:

'She openeth her mouth with wisdom; and
in her tongue is the law of kindness.'

In Memory of
JANE AUSTEN
youngest daughter of the late
Revd GEORGE AUSTEN,
formerly Rector of Steventon in this County,
she departed this Life on the 18th of July, 1817,
aged 41, after a long illness supported with
the patience and the hopes of a Christian.

The benevolence of her heart,
the sweetness of her temper, and
the extraordinary endowments of her mind
obtained the regard of all who knew her, and
the warmest love of her intimate connections.

Their grief is in proportion to their affection,
they know their loss to be irreparable,
but in their deepest affliction they are consoled
by a firm though humble hope that her charity,
devotion, faith and purity, rendered
her soul acceptable in the sight of her
REDEEMER.

On Susanna Barford who died aged ten. This epitaph was recorded by John Aubrey before 1697, but its whereabouts remain untraced.

This world to
her was but
a traged Play,
She came
and saw't,
dislikt, and
pass'd away.

Epitaph on the *grave of Sir Thomas Beecham, CH (1879–1961), the orchestral conductor. He was originally buried in Brookwood Cemetery, near Woking, but was re-interred at the parish cemetery of Limpsfield, Surrey, in April 1991. Thus he came to lie a few feet from Frederick Delius, the composer whose work he had championed (and at whose funeral he spoke and conducted in 1934).

The inscription is taken from John Fletcher's play *The False One* (written in about 1620). Beecham arranged music for several productions of Fletcher's plays and gave the Oxford Romanes Lecture on the playwright in 1956. According to *Beecham Stories* (compiled by Harold Atkins and Archie Newman, 1978), after producing Fletcher's *The Faithful Shepherdess*, Beecham received a letter from the Inland Revenue asking for the playwright's address for the purposes of taxation, as they had been unable to discover his whereabouts. 'I was able to reply that to the best of my knowledge his present residence was the South Aisle of Southwark Cathedral,' said Beecham.

NOTHING CAN COVER
HIS HIGH FAME BUT
HEAVEN. NO PYRAMIDS
SET OFF HIS MEMORIES
BUT THE ETERNAL
SUBSTANCE OF HIS
GREATNESS.

Hilaire Belloc (1870–1953) wrote this epitaph for himself in 'On his Books' (1923). He is actually buried in a family grave at the Church of Our Lady of Consolation, West Grinstead, Sussex, but, obviously, without this inscription. A few yards away, a *plaque on the tower commemorates him, noting that he had been a member of the congregation for 48 years. The tower and spire were completed in 1964, 'in grateful recognition of his zealous and unwavering profession of our Holy Faith which he defended in his writings and noble verse.' Then follow his lines from 'The Ballade of Our Lady of Czestocjowa':

'This is the Faith that I have held and hold
and This is That in which I mean to die.'

When I am dead,
I hope it may be said:
'His sins were scarlet,
but his books were read'.

There is a so far unexplained conjunction between the lyric of the song 'Don't Cry for Me, Argentina' from the Tim Rice/ Andrew Lloyd Webber musical *Evita* (1976) and the inscription (in Spanish) that appears on Eva Perón's bronze tomb at the Recoleta Cemetery, Buenos Aires. That begins with words to the effect, 'Do not cry for me when I am far away.' Eva's body was not returned to Argentina until 1976 and the inscription (of which there is more than one) in Recoleta Cemetery bears the date '1982'. Could it have been inspired by the song rather than the other way round?

The tomb also bears the words: '*Volvere y sere millones!* [I will come again, and I will be millions].' According to Nicholas Fraser, co-author of *Eva Perón* (1980), 'She never said this last, but that doesn't keep it from being true', though some sources give it as from a speech she made towards the end of her life. It was also the title of another musical written about her by Argentinean nationalists.

Volvere y sere

Eva died in 1952. Curiously, in that same year, Howard Fast published his novel *Spartacus*, in which the following appears in Chap. 1 (at the end of Pt 2), referring to a slave crucified as part of the vengeance of Rome: 'Do you know what was the last thing he said?' 'What?' whispered Claudia. '*I will return and I will be millions* [Fast's italics]. Just that. Fanciful, isn't it?'

This, if anything, is a reference to an insurrection of maltreated natives in the Peru/Bolivia area in the years 1780–2 and known as the revolt of Tupac Amarú. When on 15 November 1781, the Indian leader Tapac Katari (Julian Apaza) was going to be tortured to death, he told his enemies: '*A mi solo me mataréis, pero mañana volveré y seré millones* [me alone you will kill, but tomorrow I will return, and I will be millions].' There is, however, nothing in the documentary record that suggests he ever uttered the words but apparently they have become part of South-American revolutionary legend.

millones!

[I will come again, and I will be millions]

When it comes to the epitaphs reported from the American West, one hungers for proof that they ever actually existed. On the other hand, there is little reason to suppose that they did not ...

In Tombstone, Arizona, there is said to have been a rough-cut epitaph on a Wells Fargo agent who was gunned down:

> Here lies Lester Moore.
> Four slugs from a forty-four.
> No Les. No More.

This was included in Fritz Spiegl, *A Small Book of Grave Humour* (1971).

Compare what President Harry S Truman said in Winslow, Arizona on 15 June 1948: 'You know, the greatest epitaph in the country is here in Arizona. It's in Tombstone and says, "Here lies Jack Williams. He done his damnedest." I think that is the greatest epitaph a man could have. Whenever a man does the best he can, then that is all he can do; and that is what your President has been trying to do for the last three years for this country.'

In 1964, Truman more precisely located the epitaph in Boot Hill Cemetery, Tombstone, and said that it went on, 'What more could a person do?' He added, of himself, 'Well, that's all I could do. I did my damnedest and that's all there is to it.'

On BBC Radio *Quote...Unquote* (1 December 1981), Naomi Lewis gave this, rather, as an epitaph on a mule...

HERE LIES BILL.

HE DONE HIS DAMNEDEST

A joint celebration of a much-married pair, on a *tablet in Birdbrook Church, Haverhill, Essex, though obviously they were never married to each other. This version of the text is from Peter Haining, *Graveyard Wit* (1973). The biblical quotation (which is only of slight relevance) is from St Matthew 22:27, concerning the woman who was married to seven brothers.

MARTHA BLEWIT,
of the Swan Inn at Bathorn-End
in this Parish,
buried May 7th, 1681:
was the Wife of nine Husbands successively,
but the ninth outlived her.
The Text to her Funeral Sermon was
"Last of all the Woman died also."

ROBERT HOGAN
of this Parish
was the Husband of Seven Wives successively,
he married Ann Livermore his seventh Wife
January 1st 1739.

In Clun in Shropshire, these words are written on the *grave of the 'playwright, actor and friend', John Osborne (1929–94). They are the last lines of his play *The Entertainer* (1957), Act 3, Sc. 13, as spoken by the seedy comedian Archie Rice: 'You've been a good audience. Very good. A very *good* audience. Let me know where you're working tomorrow night – and I'll come and see YOU.' Osborne suggested 'possibly it might be my own epitaph' – and so it became. It can be seen in St George's churchyard.

⊕

JOHN
OSBORNE
PLAYWRIGHT·ACTOR
AND FRIEND

✳

12 DECEMBER 1929
24 DECEMBER 1994

**Let me know where
you're working
tomorrow night
– and I'll come
and see YOU.**

From the *tomb of Captain Bligh in the grounds of St Mary's Church, Lambeth. He earned the nickname 'Bread Fruit Bligh' on account of his discovery of that crop when accompanying Captain Cook on his voyage of 1772–4. Understandably, the inscription makes no mention of what Bligh is most notorious for: being the cause of the 1789 mutiny on his ship, HMS *Bounty*, though these days it is argued that he was not quite the tyrant as portrayed, for example, by Charles Laughton in the 1935 film of the incident. Lest modern novels and films be blamed for portraying Bligh as a tyrant, be it noted that the *Dictionary of National Biography* was writing of his 'irascible temper and overbearing conduct' as the cause of the mutiny, in 1886.

SACRED

TO THE MEMORY OF

WILLIAM BLIGH, ESQUIRE, F.R.S.

VICE ADMIRAL OF THE BLUE,

THE CELEBRATED NAVIGATOR

WHO FIRST TRANSPLANTED THE BREAD FRUIT

TREE FROM OTAHEITE TO THE WEST INDIES,

BRAVELY FOUGHT THE BATTLES OF HIS COUNTRY,

AND DIED BELOVED, RESPECTED AND LAMENTED,

ON THE 7TH DAY OF DECEMBER, 1817.

AGED 64.

Did this famously amusing epitaph ever exist? W.H. Beable, *Epitaphs: Graveyard Humour & Eulogy* (1925) has not only this one, but also a version involving 'Major James Brush ... 1831 (Woolwich Churchyard)'. Beable also finds the similar, 'Erected to the Memory of / John Phillips / Accidentally Shot / As a mark of affection by his brother'. Earlier, David Mackae, *A Pennyworth of Queer Epitaphs* (?1910) had found the same epitaph in India. One suspects it is no more than a joke and never actually appeared on a grave. *Pass the Port Again* (1980) ascribed it confidently to the grave of David Warnock in Simla.

The *Faber Book of Anecdotes* has it that James Whitcomb Riley (1849–1916), the American poet, said of a cook who had worked for a family many years, and who fell asleep over her stove and was burned to death, 'Well done, good and faithful servant'.

The phrase 'good and faithful servant' derives from Matthew 25:21 and Luke 19:17.

Here lies

Captain Ernest Bloomfield

Accidentally shot by his Orderly

March 2nd 1789

———◆———

Well done, thou good and faithful servant.

On the *memorial to Lord Byron's beloved Newfoundland dog which is buried in the gardens of Newstead Abbey, Nottinghamshire. The wording, once attributed to Byron himself, is now thought to have been written by John Cam Hobhouse, his close friend. The poet at one time intended to be buried in the same vault as the dog.

Byron's own poem dated 30 November 1808 is appended beneath the inscription and runs, in part:

When some proud Son of Man returns to Earth,
Unknown to Glory, but upheld by Birth,
The sculptor's art exhausts the pomp of woe,
And storied urns record who rests below:
When all is done, upon the Tomb is seen,
Not what he was, but what he should have been
...Ye! who perchance behold this simple urn,
Pass on – it honours none you wish to mourn:
To mark a friend's remains these stones arise;
I never knew but one – and here he lies.

Near this Spot
are deposited the Remains of one
who possessed Beauty without Vanity,
Strength without Insolence,
Courage without Ferocity,
and all the Virtues of Man without his Vices.
This praise, which would be unmeaning
Flattery,
if inscribed over human Ashes,
is but a just Tribute to the Memory of
BOATSWAIN, a *DOG*
who was born in *Newfoundland*, May 1803,
and died at *Newstead*, Nov. 18, 1808.

A Collection of Epitaphs and Monumental Inscriptions (1806) has this as coming from 'Horsley-Down Church, Cumberland'; G.W.E. Russell, *Collections and Recollections* (1898) has it 'in a churchyard in Northumberland' and as reprinted in the Annual Register. Raymond Lamont Brown, *A New Book of Epitaphs* (1973) and Peter Haining, *Graveyard Wit* (1973) both have it in 'Horsley Church, Cumberland'; 'To be found in the churchyard of Horsleydown, Cumberland' – Nancy McPhee, *The Second Book of Insults* (1981). I can find no 'Horsleydown' in that part of the world, though there are two Horsleys in Northumberland.

More convincingly, Joan Bakewell and John Drummond, *A Fine and Private Place* (1977) (who give the transcription opposite) says it is from St John, Horsleydown, Bermondsey, London. Indeed, there used to be such a church (on Tower Bridge Road) but it was gutted by bombing in the Second World War, and now has a modern building on the old foundations. A few gravestones are visible, though not, alas, this splendid one.

Here lie the bodies
Of THOMAS BOND and MARY his Wife.
She was temperate, chaste, charitable,
BUT
She was proud, peevish, and passionate.
She was an affectionate wife, and a tender mother;
BUT
Her husband and child, whom she loved,
Seldom saw her countenance without a disgusting frown,
Whilst she received visitors, whom she despised,
With an endearing smile. Her behaviour was discreet towards strangers,
BUT
Imprudent in her family.
Abroad, her conduct was influenced by good breeding
BUT
At home by ill temper. She was a professed enemy to flattery,
And was seldom known to praise or commend;
BUT
The talents in which she principally excelled
Were difference of opinion, and discovering flaws and imperfections.
She was an admirable economist, and, without prodigality,
Dispensed plenty to every person in her family;
BUT
Would sacrifice their eyes to a farthing candle.
She sometimes made her husband happy with her good qualities;
BUT
Much more frequently miserable
With her many failings; Insomuch, that in thirty years' cohabitation,
He often lamented that maugre all her virtues
He had not, in the whole, enjoyed two years of matrimonial comfort.
AT LENGTH
Finding she had lost the affection of her husband,
As well as the regard of her neighbours,
Family disputes having been divulged by servants,
She died of vexation, July 20, 1768 aged 48.
Her worn-out husband survived her four months and two days,
And departed this life, Nov 28, 1768, aged 54.

WILLIAM BOND, Brother to the deceased,
erected this stone as a weekly monitor to the surviving
wives of this parish, that they may avoid the infamy
of having their memories handed down to posterity,
with a patch-work character.

On the *grave of Mary Broomfield, who died aged 80 in 1755, at Macclesfield in Cheshire. Text from Joan Bakewell and John Drummond, *A Fine and Private Place* (1977):

The chief concern of her life for the last twenty-five years was to order and provide for her funeral. Her greatest pleasure was to think and talk about it. She lived many years on a pension of 9d per week, and yet she saved £5, which at her own request was laid out on her funeral.

'I found this delightful epitaph on a tombstone in Winchester. Can any of us hope to do more?' asked Clarissa Palmer (2004). Consequently, Alice J. McCabe of Doncaster gently reprimanded me for finding it ever so slightly curious. It is, or could have been meant to be, a biblical quotation. In St Mark 14:8, Jesus says it of the woman who anointed his body. In the Authorized Version, it is 'She hath wrought a good work on me' but in the New International Version it is indeed, 'She did what she could.' In fact, this is quite a common text on gravestones. John Pepperdine commented that this may be because 'She hath done what she could' was used as the subtitle of a Victorian treatise by Aldert Smedes (1810–77) on 'The duty and responsibility of woman'.

In loving memory of my dear wife

Annie Edith Faithfull

1877–1954

'SHE DID WHAT SHE COULD'

'On a Dentist' – in Robin Hyman, *A Dictionary of Famous Quotations* (1967). Peter Haining, *Graveyard Wit* (1973) has a similar rhyme more precisely from 'St George's Church, Edinburgh'.

Stranger! Approach this spot with gravity! John Brown is filling his last cavity.

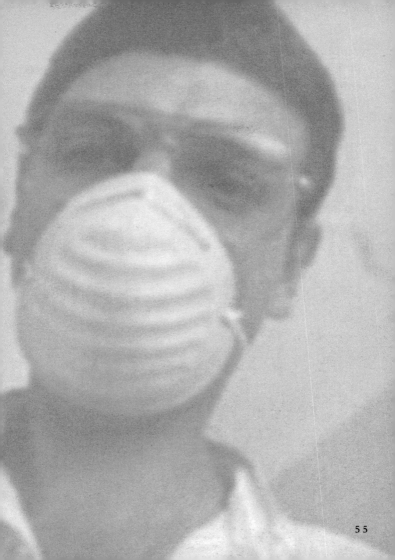

W. Fairley, *Epitaphiana* (1875) and W.H. Beable, *Epitaphs: Graveyard Humour & Eulogy* (1925) both have this, the latter noting 'a distinctly American flavour'. William Tegg, *Epitaphs, Witty, Grotesque, Elegant &c.* (1876) has the similar:

> Underneath this ancient pew
> Lie the remains of Jonathan Blue;
> His name was Black, but that wouldn't do.

Compare the epitaph on Jessica Jones (page 135).

HERE LIES JOHN BUNN

WHO WAS KILLED BY A GUN.

HIS NAME WASN'T BUN,

HIS REAL NAME WAS WOOD,

BUT WOOD WOULDN'T RHYME WITH GUN,

SO I THOUGHT BUNN SHOULD.

This epitaph concerns the leading Elizabethan actor, Richard Burbage (?1567–1619), who was a colleague of William Shakespeare. Burbage probably died of the plague and was buried at St Leonard's, Shoreditch, as was his father, James, who built the first London theatre in 1576. What Richard's actual epitaph (if any) was, is not known (the present church is of more recent vintage), though several poetic epitaphs on him survive. The suggested one opposite, that has been called the 'briefest epitaph on any man', first appeared in William Camden, 'Remains' (1674 edition):

Burbage.

Admiral Byng (1704–57) was executed at Portsmouth after failing to relieve Minorca, giving rise to Voltaire's comment in *Candide* (1759) that in England it was 'thought well to kill an admiral from time to time to encourage the others'. This *inscription can be found in a vault belonging to the Torrington family in the church of All Saints, Southill, Bedfordshire.

To The Perpetual Disgrace
of PUBLICK JUSTICE
The Honble JOHN BYNG Esqr
Admiral of the Blue
Fell a MARTYR to
POLITICAL PERSECUTION
March *14th* in the Year *1757* when
BRAVERY and LOYALTY
Were Insufficient Securities
For the
Life and Honour
of a
NAVAL OFFICER

This much-recalled epitaph may be found in *A Collection of Epitaphs and Monumental Inscriptions* (1806). According to the guidebook (1982) of the church at St Ewe, near St Austell, Cornwall, it 'unfortunately cannot now be found, but was inscribed on an 18th Century headstone'. Joan Bakewell and John Drummond, *A Fine and Private Place* (1977) give the version as here as though from St Agnes, which is on the north coast of Cornwall, near Redruth. However, St Agnes is nearer to St Columb, if that is relevant.

Here lies the body of Joan Carthew,

Born at St. Columb, buried at St. Kew.

Children she had five,

Three are dead, and two alive.

Those that are dead chusing rather

To die with their Mother

Than live with their Father.

In an undated newspaper cutting (possibly from the early 1900s), 'C.W.' writes: 'While lately strolling through an old Surrey church containing altar-tombs, escutcheons and memorials of the House of Exeter, [this] epitaph on a large marble slab, suspended high in the mortuary chapel, arrested my attention. It is printed in uncials, and I reproduce the arrangement in facsimile.'

Dorothy Cecil
Unmarried
As Yet.

A Collection of Epitaphs and Monumental Inscriptions (1806) has this from 'St Luke's, Chelsea'. The present church built in the 1820s does not appear to contain any remnant of the inscription, even among the many old stones arranged round St Luke's Gardens.

Sacred to posterity.

In a vault, near this place, lies the body of

ANNE, the only daughter of
EDWARD CHAMBERLAYNE, LL.D.
Born in London, January 20, 1667,
Who,
For a considerable time, declined the matrimonial state,
And scheming many things
Superior to her sex and age,
On the 30th of June, 1690,
And under the command of her brother,
With the arms and in the dress of a man,
She approv'd herself a true VIRAGO,
By fighting undaunted in a fire ship against the French,
Upwards of six hours.
She might have given us a race of heroes,
Had not premature fate interposed.
She returned safe from that naval engagement,
And was married, in some months after, to
JOHN SPRAGGE, Esq.
With whom she lived half a year extremely happy,
But being delivered of a daughter, she died
A few days after,

October 30, 1692.

This monument, to his most dear and affectionate wife, was
erected by her most disconsolate husband.

Raymond Lamont Brown, *A New Book of Epitaphs* (1973) has this 'from the US'. Compare:

Here lie the bones of Elizabeth Charlotte,
That was born a virgin and died a harlot.
She was aye a virgin till seventeen –
An extraordinary thing for Aberdeen.

– quoted in Donald and Catherine Carswell,
The Scots Week-End (1936).

Here lies the bones of Copperstone Charlotte

Born a virgin, died a harlot.

For sixteen years she kep' her virginity

A damn'd long time in this vicinity.

A gloriously detailed epitaph on a *grave in the Roman Catholic cemetery, Beaconsfield, Buckinghamshire.

IN LOVING REMEMBRANCE

OF

ALFRED JOPLING COOPER

(COMMODORE OF THE P.S.N. CO.)

WHO PASSED AWAY NOV:16TH 1923:
ON THE EVE OF HIS 76TH BIRTHDAY.

HE DISCOVERED THE SOLECTRIC THEORY WHICH
ENABLES US TO UNDERSTAND THE FORCES WHICH
ARE ACTING TO CAUSE NATURAL PHENOMENA,
EARTHQUAKES, VIOLENT STORMS, TORNADOES, ETC.

THE NEGATIVE CIRCLE OF INTENSE SOLECTRIC FORCE
HAS A RADIUS ON EARTH'S SURFACE OF $57\frac{1}{2}°$:
THE POSITIVE CIRCLE HAS A RADIUS OF 88°.

HE PREDICTED THE VALPARAISO EARTHQUAKE
OF AUG:16:1906, AND HE ALSO PREDICTED IN THE
VALPARAISO "MERCURIO" OF OCT:10: AS CONFIRMED
IN PAGE 7 OF "THE TIMES" OF DEC:7:1918, THE
DAY AND HOUR OF THE CHILIAN EARTHQUAKE
OF DEC:4:1918, HENCE 8 WEEKS BEFORE ITS
OCCURRENCE.

On the horse's *grave in the Ice House Paddock at Stratfield Saye House (the 1st Duke of Wellington's country home), where the chestnut stallion had spent a long retirement and was buried with full military honours.

HERE LIES

COPENHAGEN

THE CHARGER RIDDEN BY
THE DUKE OF WELLINGTON
THE ENTIRE DAY, AT THE
BATTLE OF WATERLOO

BORN 1808 DIED 1836

GOD'S HUMBLER INSTRUMENT,
THOUGH MEANER CLAY,
SHOULD SHARE THE GLORY
OF THAT GLORIOUS DAY.

This memorial *tablet is to be found in Kensal Green Cemetery, London. George Cruikshank only lay here for a few months before his remains were moved to the crypt of St Paul's Cathedral, but his widow evidently felt it necessary to erect this stone giving more space to his work as an abstainer than to his achievement as an artist. In his youth Cruikshank had been addicted to gin. In 1847 he had great success with a series of drawings called *The Bottle* which showed the degradation of a family through drink. He then became a total abstainer himself.

A bust and other ornaments have been removed from the memorial. The widow herself is apparently buried at this spot. Note the helpful address. Mrs Cruikshank also wrote and signed the *epitaph in St Paul's. It is on the wall near the floor slab covering his grave, refrains from mentioning his temperance work, and concludes:

> In Memory of his Genius and his Art
> His matchless Industry and worthy work
> For all his fellow-men. This Monument
> Is humbly placed within this sacred Fane
> By her who loved him best, his widowed wife.

What is left unmentioned in all this is the fact that Cruikshank had no children by his legal wife and only after his death did she discover that he had set up a former housemaid in premises only a few streets away from the marital home, by whom he had had several children.

In Loving Memory

OF

GEORGE CRUIKSHANK

ARTIST

DESIGNER, ETCHER, PAINTER

BORN SEPT 27TH 1792

DIED FEB 1ST 1878

AT 263 HAMPSTEAD RD, LONDON

AGED 86

FOR 30 YEARS A TOTAL ABSTAINER
AND ARDENT PIONEER AND CHAMPION
BY PENCIL, WORD AND PEN,
OF UNIVERSAL ABSTINENCE
FROM INTOXICATING DRINKS ...

THIS MONUMENT IS ERECTED
BY HIS AFFECTIONATE WIDOW
ELIZA CRUIKSHANK.

'From Nevern – translated from the Welsh' – quoted by
Wynford Vaughan-Thomas (1982).

Deep in this grave
lies lazy Dai
Waiting the last great trump
on high.
If he's as fond of his grave
as he's fond of his bed
He'll be the last man up
when that roll call's said.

A Collection of Epitaphs and Monumental Inscriptions (1806) has this from 'Shrewsbury church-yard'.

HERE LIES THE BODY OF
MARTHA DIAS,
WHO WAS ALWAYS UNEASY,
AND NOT OVER PIOUS.
SHE LIV'D TO THE AGE OF
THREESCORE AND TEN,
AND GAVE THAT TO THE WORMS
SHE REFUS'D TO THE MEN.

From a memorial *tablet to Robert Cadman on the exterior wall of the tower of St Mary's Church, St Mary's Street, Shrewsbury. The 'Sabrine stream' is the River Severn which flows through Shrewsbury ('Sabrina' being a Romano-British name for that river).

Let this small Monument record the name
Of CADMAN, and to future times proclaim
How by'n attempt to fly from this high spire
Across the Sabrine stream he did acquire
His fatal end. 'Twas not for want of skill
Or courage to perform the task he fell:
No, no, a faulty Cord being drawn too tight
Hurried his Soul on high to take her flight
Which bid the Body here beneath good Night:
Febry 2nd 1739 aged 28.

Part of the tablet in York Minster commemorating
Viscountess Downe who died in 1812. According to
J.B. Morrell, *The Biography of the Common Man of the City
of York* (1948), these words are preceded by an account of
her ancestry and family connections.

As for the last sentence, it is not uncommon in epitaphs.
Compare, from David Mackae, *A Pennyworth of Queer
Epitaphs* (?1910):

> Here lie several of the Stows,
> Particulars the last day will disclose.

And, from Philip Reder, *Epitaphs* (1969), in Tetbury church,
Gloucestershire:

> Here lie several of the Saunderses of this Parish.
> Further particulars the last day will disclose.
> Amen.

The 18th-century epitaph on Anne Thursby, wife of John
Harvey Thursby, on the south wall of Abington Parish Church,
Northampton, includes the lines:

> What Sort of Woman She Was
> The Last Day Will Determine.

A real unpretending and almost unconscious good sense and a firm desire to act right on all occasions to the best of her judgment were her most distinguished characteristics, hereditary personal grace of both form and face which even in age had not disappeared completes her picture. For her character and other particulars see the Gentleman's Magazine for May, 1812.

In 2002, Ken and Linda Brockway (who run a local history website from near Nottingham) asked if I could help them identify an epitaph on the grave of John Handley (died 1694) in Redmile churchyard, as here. They also found the verse on the headstone of the grave of John Smith (died 1725) at Hickling, some ten miles away.

It transpired that what we have here is a blending of two quotations: the last verse of an old ballad called 'Death and the Lady' (as printed sometime between 1683 and 1700) goes:

The grave's the market place where all must meet
Both rich and poor, as well as small and great;
If life were merchandise, that gold could buy,
The rich would live – only the poor would die.

And in the play *Two Noble Kinsmen* (?1613), thought to be a collaboration between Shakespeare and John Fletcher, the end of Act 1 Sc. 5 is as follows:

Third Queen: This funeral path brings to your household's grave –
Joy seize on you again, peace sleep with him.
Second Queen: And this to yours.
First Queen: Yours this way. Heavens lend
A thousand differing ways to one sure end.
Third Queen: This world's a city full of straying streets,
And death's the market-place where each one meets.
  [*Exeunt severally*]

Then, beneath the entry for this in Benham's *Book of Quotations* (1948), I found a footnote: 'At Nutfield churchyard, Surrey, England, is a stone in memory of Henry Devall, d. Dec 18, 1860, aged 73,' with these lines:

This world's a city with many a crooked street,
And Death the Market place where all men meet.
If Life were merchandise that men could buy,
The rich would live and none but the poor would die.

This world it is a city full of crooked streets

Death is a market place where all men meet.

If life were marchandice that men could buy

Rich men would ever live and poor men die.

Natasha Coombs wrote (2003): 'While doing research for my dissertation, in Aron's Vale Cemetery, Bristol, I found a most unusual headstone in the form of a piece of machinery. It was dedicated to the memory of 'a clever engineer'. Even better was that among the engineer's descendants named on the stone was his grandson who died in 1919. He was commemorated with the following quote':

We have whacked the huns!

Sylvia Plath, the American-born poet who committed suicide in London in 1963, is buried in the churchyard at Heptonstall in West Yorkshire. She is described as 'SYLVIA PLATH HUGHES', although at the time of her death, she was estranged from her husband, the poet Ted Hughes. On a fairly regular basis, feminist supporters of Plath have attempted to blot out the name Hughes.

It was, indeed, Hughes who arranged for Plath's burial in his own home village and chose the somewhat obscure epitaph on her *grave. It used to be asserted that the words were a translation from the Hindu poem, 'The Bhagavad-Gita', but Hughes said in *The Guardian* (20 April 1989), that it was merely a 'translation from the Sanskrit'.

In fact, it comes from the book *Journey to the West,* also known as *Monkey,* written by Wu Ch'Eng-En in the middle of the 16th century. It is spoken by a Patriarch who is teaching Monkey the way of long life. The full quote is: 'To spare and tend the vital powers, this and nothing else is sum and total of all magic, secret and profane. All is comprised in these three, spirit, breath and soul; guard them closely, screen them well; let there be no leak. Store them within the frame; that is all that can be learnt, and all that can be taught. I would have you mark the tortoise and snake, locked in tight embrace. Locked in tight embrace, the vital powers are strong; *even in the midst of fierce flames the Golden Lotus may be planted*, the five elements compounded and transposed, and put to new use. When that is done, be which you please, Buddha or Immortal.'

Now our only question is why Hughes would refer to something authored by Wu Ch'Eng-En as 'a translation from the Sanskrit'. Anne Stevenson, author of *Bitter Fame* (1989), a Plath biography, commented in 2001: 'Its significance is obvious. Sylvia was burning in a private hell of her own for most of her short life. The golden lotus is the poetry planted in the fierce flames of Sylvia's incipient fury.'

IN MEMORY
SYLVIA PLATH HUGHES
1932 — 1963
EVEN AMIDST FIERCE FLAMES
THE GOLDEN LOTUS CAN BE PLANTED

The saying, 'There is not enough darkness in all the world to put out the light of even one small candle' is attributed by *The David & Charles Book of Quotations* (1986) to the American theologian, Robert Alden (1937–) On the other hand, Bernard Levin described it in *Conducted Tour* (1981) as 'an ancient proverb'. On yet another hand, a marmoset's *gravestone on the Oxford road out of Henley-on-Thames has it also, apparently dating from 1937. It is believed that the memorial was raised by Jimmy's owner, a Miss Doris Jekyll. If this epitaph was applied near to the date of death it would rule out Alden's claim to authorship.

JIMMY
A TINY MARMOSET
AUGUST 16TH 1937

THERE ISN'T ENOUGH
DARKNESS IN THE WORLD
TO QUENCH THE LIGHT
OF ONE SMALL CANDLE

JIMMY
A TINY MARMOSET
AUGUST 16TH 1937

THERE ISN'T ENOUGH
DARKNESS IN THE WORLD
TO EXTINGUISH THE LIGHT
OF ONE SMALL CANDLE

A curiously-chosen quotation appears split between the adjoining graves containing the ashes of the TV playwright Dennis Potter and those of his wife Margaret in St Mary's churchyard, Ross-on-Wye. Remarkably, Margaret died of cancer on 27 May 1994 and Dennis followed her on the 7 June, also of cancer. Apart from their dates, no description is given of them. A quotation from Alice Hoffman's novel *Turtle Moon* (1992) is split between the two gravestones – 'All the way to heaven is heaven' on Margaret's and 'All of it a kiss' on Dennis's. Humphrey Carpenter in his biography of Potter (1999) quotes Sarah, their daughter, as saying that *Turtle Moon* was a book Margaret read and loved. Sarah goes on: 'Dad didn't actually care for [the epitaph] very much, but he said, "We'll do what your mother wants".'

All of it a kiss

Another curiously-chosen quotation is to be found on the *grave of the creator of Sherlock Holmes in All Saints' churchyard, Minstead, Hampshire. The quotation comes from Robert Louis Stevenson's poem 'My Wife' in *Songs of Travel* (1896):

> Steel-true and blade-straight
> The great artificer
> Made my mate.

Presumably, 'my wife' chose the epitaph.

STEEL TRUE
BLADE STRAIGHT

ARTHUR CONAN DOYLE
KNIGHT
PATRIOT, PHYSICIAN & MAN OF LETTERS
22 MAY 1859 – 7 JULY 1930
AND HIS BELOVED, HIS WIFE
JEAN CONAN DOYLE
REUNITED 27 JUNE 1940

An epitaph from the burial ground near the present Anglican Cathedral in Liverpool, recalled by the novelist Beryl Bainbridge on BBC Radio *Quote...Unquote* (29 June 1988). She said that another in the same place, on a certain 'G. Wild', bore the words, 'Not worth remembering'.

John Edwards
who perished in
a fire 1904.

None could hold
a candle to him.

What W.C. Fields (1880–1946), the American comedian, actually submitted as a suggested epitaph, when asked to do so by *Vanity Fair* magazine in 1925, was: 'Here lies W.C. Fields. I would rather be living in Philadelphia.' There had apparently been an earlier expression, 'Sooner dead than in Philadelphia'. To Fields is also attributed the snubbing remark, 'I went to Philadelphia and found it was closed.' There is no reference to the city on his actual tombstone. It simply bears his name and dates.

On the whole
I'd rather be

in Philadelphia.

At first sight, one of the most delightful epitaphs of all is to be found on a *floor slab in Dorchester Abbey, Oxfordshire. Alas, the story behind the epitaph is far from delightful. Sarah Fletcher fell in love with and married Captain Fletcher, a naval officer, but after the wedding he was exposed as a bigamist, being already married to another wife in some foreign port. He left poor Sarah and went abroad to avoid punishment. The heartbreak and public disgrace of this situation was too much for her. At the age of 29, she hanged herself in her cottage at Clifton Hampden. As a suicide she would normally have been denied burial in consecrated ground, but such was the sympathy for her among her friends and family (and presumably the clergy of Dorchester) that they buried her in the abbey and the beautifully-worded epitaph, while describing the causes of her sad death, does not reveal the detail. There was no doubt real feeling behind the final line: 'May she find that peace in heaven which this life denied her.'

Reader!

If thou hast a heart fam'd for
Tenderness and Pity, Contemplate this Spot.
In which are deposited the Remains
of a Young Lady, whose artless Beauty,
innocence of Mind and gentle Manners,
once obtained her the Love and
Esteem of all who knew her, But when
Nerves were too delicately spun to
bear the rude Shakes and Jostlings
which we meet with in this transitory
World, Nature gave way; She sunk
and died a Martyr to Excessive Sensibility.

Mrs SARAH FLETCHER
Wife of Captain FLETCHER,
departed this Life at the Village
of Clifton, on the 7 of June 1799.
In the 29 Year of her Age.
May her Soul meet that Peace in
Heaven which this Earth denied her.

This punning epitaph on Samuel Foote (1720–77), actor and dramatist, famous for his mimicry and for making Samuel Johnson laugh against his will, was not, however, put on his actual grave. He was buried in Westminster Abbey cloister by torchlight and in an unmarked grave. This epitaph is recorded in *A Collection of Epitaphs and Monumental Inscriptions* (1806). Another, playing upon his role as mimic, was:

> Foote from his earthly stage, alas! is hurled;
> Death took him off, who took off all the world.

The expression 'to have one foot in the grave' means, of course, to be near death.

Here lies one Foote,
whose death may
thousands save,
For death has now one
foot within the grave.

Benjamin Franklin, the American scientist, diplomat and writer (1706–90) suggested this epitaph for himself in about 1728. William Andrews, *Curious Epitaphs* (1899) compares it to other similarly punning printers' epitaphs. *Cassell's Book of Quotations* (1907) quotes the Revd Joseph Capen (19th century), 'Lines on Mr John Foster':

Yet at the resurrection we shall see
A fair edition, and of matchless worth,
Free from erratas, new in heaven set forth.

Cassell's also suggests that the idea was borrowed from the Revd Benjamin Woodbridge, chaplain to Charles II, who wrote these 'Lines of John Cotton' (1652):

O what a monument of glorious worth,
When in a new edition he comes forth,
Without erratas, may we think he'll be
In leaves and covers of eternity!

In fact, Franklin lies with his wife under a simple inscription in Christ Church, Philadelphia: 'Benjamin and Deborah Franklin, February 1790'.

The body
of Benjamin Franklin, printer,
(Like the cover of an old book,
Its contents worn out,
And stript of its lettering and gilding)
Lies here, food for worms!
Yet the work itself shall not be lost,
For it will, as he believed, appear once more
In a new
And more beautiful edition,
Corrected and amended
By its Author!

A suggested epitaph on Frederick Louis, Prince of Wales (1707–51), eldest son of George II and father of George III, quoted by Horace Walpole in an appendix to his *Memoirs of George II* (1847). Frederick quarrelled with his father and was banished from court.

Compare *Frobisher New Select Collection of Epitaphs* (?1790), 'On a tombstone in Cornwall':

> Here lies honest Ned,
> Because he is dead.
> Had it been his father...

A Collection of Epitaphs and Monumental Inscriptions (1806) has 'from a headstone in the church-yard of Storrington in the County of Sussex':

> Here lies the body of Edward Hide;
> We laid him here because he died.
> We had rather it had been his father.
> If it had been his sister,
> We should not have miss'd her.
> But since 'tis honest Ned
> No more shall be said...

Peter Haining, *Graveyard Wit* (1973) has a version beginning 'Here lies HONEST NED... ' from 'Kirkby Stephen parish church, Westmorland'.

Here lies Fred,
Who was alive and is dead:
Had it been his father,
I had much rather;
Had it been his brother,
Still better than another;
Had it been his sister
No one would have missed her;
Had it been the whole
generation,
Still better for the nation:
But since 'tis only Fred,
Who was alive and is dead, -
There's no more to be said.

Charles Frohman (1860–1915) was an influential theatrical producer in Britain and America. He it was who first presented J.M. Barrie's *Peter Pan* (1904). He went down on the *Lusitania*. The *fountain monument near the church (but outside the churchyard) of All Saints', Marlow, Buckinghamshire, shows a nude marble maiden, and the inscription runs round the base. J. Camp in *Portrait of Buckinghamshire* (1972) comments: 'His memorial is a graceful tribute to the female form, and a reminder of the pleasure his stage presentations gave to so many on both sides of the Atlantic in late Victorian and Edwardian days.'

The text is taken from a translation of the dying words of Sappho, the Greek lyric poet of the late 7th century BC – also sometimes rendered as 'For it is not right that in the house of song...'

Frohman's body was recovered from the sea and a funeral was held for him in New York (according to a 1916 biography by I.F. Marcosson and D. Frohman). His 'last words' were reported by a survivor from the *Lusitania* as having been 'Why fear death? It is the most beautiful adventure of life' – alluding to Peter Pan's 'To die will be an awfully big adventure'.

Frohman used to spend weekends at Marlow and, indeed, expressed a wish to die and be buried there.

FOR IT IS NOT RIGHT THAT IN A HOUSE THE
MUSES HAUNT MOURNING SHOULD DWELL
– SUCH THINGS BEFIT US NOT.

Part of the inscription on the pedestal of the monument to the dramatist and poet John Gay (1685–1732). It used to be in the South Transept of Westminster Abbey but has now been moved to the Triforium. The lines were written by Gay himself, author of the hugely successful *The Beggar's Opera*. On the grave of Caleb Gould, a Thames lock-keeper (who died in 1836), in Remenham churchyard, Oxfordshire, the same epitaph is written in the form: 'This world's a jest, and all things show it. I thought so once, but now I know it.'

Life is a jest, and all things show it;
I thought so once; and now I know it.

'My father maintained that in the Vale of Aylesbury about 1900 he encountered this epitaph ... I'm afraid it was apocryphal' – E.J. Burdon, Preston, Lancs. (1982).

Here lies the body of Charlotte Greer,

Whose mouth would stretch

from ear to ear.

Be careful as you tread this sod

For if she gapes, you're gone, by God!

Quoted on BBC Radio *Quote...Unquote* (22 December 1981), but untraced.

Jonathan Grober

Died dead sober.

Lord thy wonders never cease.

In Cambridge – according to W. Fairley, *Epitaphiana* (1875); in St Alban's, Hertfordshire – according to J. Potter Briscoe, *Gleanings From God's Acre* (1901).

Here lies the body of Mary Gwynne,

Who was so very pure within,

She cracked the shell of her earthly skin,

And hatched herself a cherubim.

A plaque at Symphony Hall, Boston, Massachusetts. According to John Julius Norwich, *More Christmas Crackers* (1990), the same names are recorded on a plaque in the Philharmonic Hall, Liverpool, with this inscription: 'Members of the band on board the "Titanic". They bravely continued playing to soothe the anguish of their fellow passengers until the ship sank in the deep ... Courage and Compassion joined make the hero and the man complete.'

In Memory of
the Devoted Musicians
Wallace Henry Hartley, Bandmaster
John Fredrick Preston Clark
Percy Cornelius Taylor
John Wesley Woodward
W. Theodore Brailey
John Law Hume
Georges Krins
Roger Bricoux

Who were drowned
Still playing
As the Titanic went down
April 15, 1912.

'From a tomb in the parish churchyard of Llangeler, 15 miles north of Carmarthen' – S.C.L. Phillips, Llandysul, Dyfed (1982).

To the memory of
John Havard Esq.,
Surgeon,
who died ... 1840.
He will be long deplored
by an extensive circle of
relations and friends,
and his medical talents
had rendered him
peculiarly useful in the
neighbourhood.

'I came across this many years ago in Hemel Hempstead' –
N. Currer-Briggs, Riberac, France (1981).

In loving memory of my beloved wife, Hester, the mother of Edward, Richard, Mary, Penelope, John, Henry, Michael, Susan, Emily, Charlotte, Amelia, George, Hugh, Hester, Christopher and Daniel.

She was a great breeder of pugs, a devoted mother and a dear friend.

When the former Prime Minister, Harold Wilson, took his peerage and became Lord Wilson of Rievaulx, he chose as his motto: '*Tempus Rerum Imperator* [Time is the ruler of all things].' This is the motto of the Worshipful Company of Clockmakers of London (founded in 1631) and is written beneath its armorial bearings. Wilson was a member of the company and, according to Lady Wilson, requested that the motto be put on the headstone of his grave. Accordingly, the man who famously remarked 'A week is a long time in politics' (which might best be understood as 'timing is everything') is appropriately buried in the old church of the old town of St Mary's, one of the Isles of Scilly, under the inscription:

Tempus rerum

Imperator

In the summer of 1718, Alexander Pope and John Gay persuaded Lord Harcourt – whose house was in the village of Stanton Harcourt, Oxfordshire – to erect a monument with an epitaph by Pope over the grave of the 'Stanton Harcourt Lovers'. Gay's version is referred to in Goldsmith's *The Vicar of Wakefield* (1766).

Pope's epitaph (of which more than one version exists) was put on the *tablet in this form:

> Think not by rigorous judgment seiz'd,
> A Pair so faithful could expire;
> Victims so pure, Heav'n saw well pleas'd
> And snatch'd them in caelestial fire.
>
> Live well & fear no sudden fate
> When God calls virtue to the grave
> Alike 'tis Justice, soon or late -
> Mercy alike to kill or save.
>
> Virtue unmov'd can hear the Call,
> And face the Flash that melts the Ball.

Pope showed several epitaphs on the same couple to Lady Mary Wortley Montagu, including this other:

> Here lye two poor Lovers, who had the mishap
> Tho very chaste people, to die of a Clap.

NEAR THIS PLACE LIE THE BODIES OF
JOHN HEWET AND SARAH DREW,
AN INDUSTRIOUS YOUNG MAN AND
VIRTUOUS MAIDEN
OF THIS PARISH
CONTRACTED IN MARRIAGE
WHO BEING WITH MANY OTHERS
AT HARVEST
WORK, WERE BOTH IN
ONE INSTANT KILLED
BY LIGHTNING ON THE
LAST DAY OF JULY
1718.

'In Belturbet Churchyard, Ireland' – W. Fairley, *Epitaphiana* (1875).

HERE LIES JOHN HIGLEY WHOSE FATHER AND MOTHER WERE DROWNED IN THE PASSAGE FROM AMERICA. HAD THEY BOTH LIVED, THEY WOULD HAVE BEEN BURIED HERE.

'A plaque on the wall of the north aisle of Norwich Cathedral commemorates the Rt. Revd George Horne, D.D., President of Magdalen College, Oxford, Dean of Canterbury and Bishop of Norwich ... Died 1792' – John Julius Norwich, *Christmas Crackers* (1980).

... In Whose Character
Depths of Learning,
Brightness of Imagination,
Sanctity of Manners and
Sweetness of Temper
Were United beyond the
Usual Lot of Mortality ...
His Commentary on the Psalms
will continue to be
a Companion to the Closet
Till the Devotion of Earth shall
end in the Hallelujahs of Heaven.

'From America, I think' – A. Bune, Cambridge (1982).

In joyous memory of
George Jones
who was president of
the Newport Rifle Club
for twenty years.
'Always missed'.

In the Church of the Holy Cross in Haltwhistle, Northumberland, there is a memorial stone with the following inscription:

Post Vitem Brevem
Difficilem Inutilem
Hoc Quiescit in Domino
Robertus Teddell
... 1735, Aetatis 32.

Which being translated, reads:

After a short difficult

and useless life

Here rests in the Lord,

Robert Tweddle ...

1735,

at the age of 32.

This is but one form of the 'forced rhyme' epitaph. The earliest I have come across occurs in the diary of Edward Lear (entry for 20 April 1887):

> Below the high Cathedral stairs,
> Lie the remains of Agnes Pears.
> Her name was Wiggs; it was not Pears.
> But Pears was put to rhyme with stairs.

With 'Susan Pares' replacing 'Agnes Pears', the rhyme was first published without date in *Queery Leary Nonsense* (1911), edited from manuscripts by Lady Constance Strachey.

I have an undated newspaper cutting (probably from the early 1900s) which states that the following version was to be found in the 'burying-ground of Evandale, Tasmania':

> Beneath these monumental stones
> Lies the body of Mary Jones.
> N.B.
> Her name was Smith, it wasn't Jones,
> But Jones was put in to rhyme with stones.

Aubrey Stewart, *English Epigrams and Epitaphs* (1897) has substantially this version – with 'Lloyd', not 'Smith' – from Launceston, Tasmania.

Here lies the body of Jessica Jones
Who died of eating cherry stones.
Her name was Smith; it was not Jones;
But Jones was put to rhyme with Stones.

Adjacent epitaphs that used to be quoted by Lt Commander D. Gill Jones in his talk 'A quiet hour among the dead' (mid-20th century).

Here lies the body of Mary,
wife of John Jones of this parish.

Here lies the body of Martha,
wife of John Jones of this parish.

Here lies the body of Jane,
wife of John Jones of this parish.

John Jones. At rest.

The July 2002 newsletter of the Classical Association contained a letter from H.H. Huxley: 'On the Cambridgeshire tombstone [no more precise than this] of Fyge Jauncey (1736–1812), one may just decipher a remarkable elegiac couplet, unparalleled as an example of polyptoton (many cases of the same word). [It translates as:] "Had not the Death of Death [i.e. Christ] given death to death by his own death, closed would have been the door of everlasting life ... "'

MORS MORTIS
MORTI
MORTEM
NISA MORTE
DEDISSET,
AERTERNAE
VITAE JANUA
CLAUSA
FORET.

William Kent, who died on 4 September 1640, is buried at St Nicholas Church, Islip, Oxfordshire. This text is from Patricia Utechin, *Epitaphs from Oxfordshire* (1980). The same rhyme has also been found at St Leonard's Church, Waterstock, Oxfordshire, and – by Joan Bakewell and John Drummond, *A Fine and Private Place* (1977) – in a very old *inscription from St Eadburgha's Church, Broadway, Worcestershire:

*As thow
art so was
I. As I am
So shalt
Thou Bee.*

*As I was so are
Ye, and as I am
So shall ye bee.*

The catchphrase 'Meredith, we're in!' originated as a shout of triumph in a music-hall sketch called 'The Bailiff' (or 'Moses and Son') performed by Fred Kitchen (his dates sometimes given as 1872–1950), leading comedian with Fred Karno's company. The sketch was first seen in about 1907. The catchphrase was used each time a bailiff and his assistant looked like gaining entrance to a house. Appropriately (or not), Kitchen has the phrase on his *gravestone in West Norwood Cemetery, south London.

FRED KITCHEN ...

PASSED AWAY APRIL 1ST 1951

AGED 77 YEARS

BELOVED BY ALL WHO KNEW HIM

MEREDITH, WE'RE IN

This verse was occasioned by the death of Sir Henry Lee (1530–?1610), a courtier of Queen Elizabeth I. John Aubrey records that Lee had a monument at the foot of which his mistress's effigy was placed and that, in consequence, 'some bishop did threaten to have this monument defaced'. According to the *Dictionary of National Biography*, 'in his later years, he carried on an amour with Anne Vavasour, daughter of Henry Vavasour of Copmanthorpe, Yorkshire; she is said in her epitaph to be buried in the same grave as Lee.'

Whatever happened, Lee's monument no longer exists, though it used to be in St Peter's Church, Quarrendon, Buckinghamshire. The inscription on it concluded thus: 'In 1611, having served five succeeding princes and kept himself right and steady in many dangerous shocks and three utter turns of state, with body bent to earth and a mind erected to heaven, aged 80, knighted 60 years, he met his long attended end.' The tablet is now preserved at Hartwell House, Buckinghamshire.

The verse may possibly have led to the Dublin graffiti rhyme as quoted by Oliver St John Gogarty in *As I Was Going Down Sackville Street* (1937):

Here lies the grave of Keelin,
And on it is wife is kneeling;
If he were alive, she would be lying,
And he would be kneeling

Here lies the good old Knight Sir Harry,

Who loved well, but would not marry;

While he lived, and had his feeling,

She did lye, and he was kneeling,

Now he's dead and cannot feele

He doeth lye and shee doeth kneele.

William Andrews, *Curious Epitaphs* (1899) has this 'on a tombstone in Bury St Edmunds Cathedral'.

Reader
Pause at this Humble Stone
it Records
The fall of unguarded Youth
By the allurements of vice,
and the treacherous snares
of Seduction
SARAH LLOYD
on the 23d. of April 1800,
in the 22d Year of her Age,
Suffered a Just but ignominious
Death
for admitting her abandoned seducer
into the Dwelling House of
her Mistress,
in the Night of 3d Oct
1799,
and becoming the Instrument
in his Hands of the crimes
of Robbery and House-burning.
These were her last Words:
May my example, be a
warning to Thousands.

'In Burlington Churchyard', according to W.H. Beable, *Epitaphs: Graveyard Humour & Eulogy*, (1925); Diprose's *Book of Epitaphs* (1879) had earlier put 'Burlington, Mass.'

Here lies the body of Mary Ann Lowder,
She burst while drinking a seidlitz powder.
Called from the world to her heavenly rest,
She should have waited till it effervesced.

W.H. Beable, *Epitaphs: Graveyard Humour & Eulogy* (1925) has this possibly apocryphal inscription, referring to a river in the centre of Edinburgh.

Erected to the memory of
John MacFarlane
Drowned in the Water of Leith
By a few affectionate friends.

'On the last resting place of an Army mule somewhere in France' – J.H.A. Dick, Currie, Midlothian (1981).

IN MEMORY OF
MAGGIE
WHO IN HER TIME KICKED
TWO COLONELS,
FOUR MAJORS,
TEN CAPTAINS,
TWENTY-FOUR
LIEUTENANTS,
FORTY-TWO SERGEANTS,
FOUR HUNDRED AND
THIRTY-TWO OTHER RANKS
AND
ONE MILLS BOMB.

Quoted by Naomi Lewis (1981). It seems to have been a Victorian epitaph from an unidentified pets' cemetery.

Born a dog.

Died a gentleman.

MARQUISE ET TONY
A LA
PRINCESSE LOBANOF

'In a North Devon churchyard' – D. Whitmore, Liphook, Hants. (1982).

Robin Hyman, *A Dictionary of Famous Quotations* (1967) has:

> Mary Ann has gone to rest,
> Safe at last on Abraham's breast,
> Which may be nuts for Mary Ann,
> But is certainly rough on Abraham.

Here lies the body of Mary Anne
Safe in the arms of Abraham.
All very well for Mary Anne
But how about poor Abraham?

'Upon the Death of Sir Albertus Morton's Wife' by Sir Henry Wotton (1568–1639). Sir Albertus died in 1625, and was the poet's nephew. *A Collection of Epitaphs and Monumental Inscriptions* (1806) has it as 'Sir Albertus Moreton' and as 'he first departed; she for one day try'd'.

He first deceas'd;

To live without him

she for a little tri'd

lik'd it not, and di'd.

These lines were written by Lynn S. Maury of the Ivor Novello Memorial Society who mounted an eight-year campaign to have a plaque placed in St Paul's Cathedral crypt. On the *memorial tablet to the composer and actor, Ivor Novello (1893–1951), her monogram is attached to the words.

Novello's ashes, appropriately for the composer of 'We'll Gather Lilacs', were placed under a lilac tree in the gardens of Golders Green Crematorium, London. At his funeral there, Edward Marsh produced as an epitaph his own translation of La Fontaine:

> Some few there be, spoilt darlings of high Heaven,
> To whom the magic grace of charm is given.

On another *memorial plaque to Novello in St Paul's Church, Covent Garden, are these words, slightly adapted from Shakespeare, *The Merchant of Venice* (Act 3, Sc. 2, line 294): 'The dearest friend, the kindest man, the best-conditioned and unwearied spirit in doing courtesies.'

Blaze of lights
and music calling,
Music weeping,
rising, falling,
Like a rare &
precious diamond
His brilliance still
lives on.

Said to be in Bideford – according to J.L. Carr's pictorial map of Devon.

IN
Memory of
HANNAH CLEMENTINA BRITTON
wife of
Benjamin Candee
Born in Oxford, Conn.
Mar. 15, 1788.
Died in New Haven,
Dec. 18, 1851.
Æ. 63 yrs. & 9 mo.

HERE LIES MARY SEXTON
WHO PLEASED MANY MEN
AND NE'ER VEXED ONE

(NOT LIKE HER
UNDER THE NEXT STONE).

This is the form of a rhyme to be found in *Bartlett's Familiar Quotations* (1968) but which comes in several versions, including:

> Here lies the body of Edmund Gray
> Who died maintaining his right of way.
> He was right – dead right – as he drove along.
> But he's just as dead as if he'd been wrong.

– quoted by Sir Huw Wheldon (1981). There is also one to 'Timothy Jay', as in 'jay-walking'. A suggested rather than actual epitaph, of course.

This is the grave of Mike O'Day

Who died maintaining his right of way.

His right was clear, his will was strong.

But he's just as dead as if he'd been wrong.

165

Self-composed epitaph on John O'Hara (1905–70), the US novelist and playwright, in Princeton Cemetery, New Jersey. An 'astonishing claim', according to Brendan Gill in *Here at the New Yorker* (1975), who reports it.

Better than
anyone else, he
told the truth
about his time,
the first half of
the twentieth
century. He was
a professional.
He wrote
honestly and well.

A Collection of Epitaphs and Monumental Inscriptions (1806) found this in Bunhill Fields Cemetery, London, where it is still, although one or two of the letters are now illegible. The two parts of the *inscription are on panels at either end of the tomb.

Compare this death notice from *The Gentleman's Magazine*, May 1732: 'The wife of Walter Newberry, merchant of Gracechurch Street, in the 33rd year of her age, of the Dropsy, for which from the Year 1728 she had been tapped 57 times, and had taken from her 240 gallons of water.' Such medical-statistical epitaphs seem to have been common about this time.

HERE LYES DAME MARY PAGE
RELICT OF SIR GREGORY PAGE, BART
SHE DEPARTED THIS LIFE MARCH 4, 1728
IN THE 56 YEAR OF HER AGE.

IN 67 MONTHS SHE WAS TAPD 66 TIMES
HAD TAKEN AWAY 240 GALLONS OF WATER
WITHOUT EVER REPINING AT HER CASE
OR EVER FEARING THE OPERATION.

'On an old lady who had suffered from an ulcerated leg'
– quoted by Lt Commander D. Gill Jones in his talk 'A quiet
hour among the dead' (mid-20th century).

Here lies the body of
Who never had issue
So great was her art,
While one leg kept still

Dame Margaret Pegg
except in her leg
so deep was her cunning,
the other kept running.

I first saw this written on a *gravestone in the main avenue of Brompton Cemetery, London, in 1978 and considered it a little ungenerous even then. It is attached to the memorial for Margaret, widow of General John Lysaght Pennefather GCB. He died in 1872 and she followed in 1880. 'Better than what?', one is tempted to ask. In fact, it is quite a common biblical tag and the allusion is to St Paul's Epistle to the Philippians (1:23) where Paul compares the folly of living with the wisdom of dying: 'For I am in a strait betwixt the two, having a desire to depart, and to be with Christ; which is far better.'

"WITH CHRIST, WHICH IS FAR

BETTER."

Epitaph on the wife of Isaac Pitman (knighted 1894, died 1897). The inventor of Pitman's shorthand system, composed it in this way to demonstrate his interest in spelling reform. The text is from Peter Haining, *Graveyard Wit* (1973) which says it is in Lansdown Cemetery, Bath. Sir Isaac is himself commemorated by a plaque in the North Aisle of Bath Abbey, but the inscription is not in phonetic English.

In memori ov

MERI PITMAN

Weif ov Mr Eizak Pitman

Fonetik Printer, ov this Siti.

Died 19 August 1857, edjed 64.

"Preper tu mit thei God."

–Emos 4-12.

Dacre Balsdon in *Oxford Life* (1957) says of this *plaque in the cloister below the Cathedral, Christ Church, Oxford: 'Reflect, as you read it, that when a memorial can be erected to a Dean of Christ Church praising him for the honest attention which he paid to the Duties of his Station, the social revolution in England will have been accomplished.'

In Memory of William Pound,
many years one of the Porters of this College,
who, by an exemplary Life and Behaviour,
and an honest attention
to the Duties of his Station,
deserved and obtained
the approbation and esteem
of the whole Society.
1787

Part of the inscription on a *commemorative shield in the North Choir Aisle of the nave, Westminster Abbey. Henry Purcell (?1658–95), the composer (and Abbey organist), is also commemorated by a Latin inscription on his gravestone nearby.

In *A Pennyworth of Queer Epitaphs* (?1910), David Mackae tells the story of the widow of a fireworks manufacturer who was so impressed by Purcell's epitaph that she caused to be placed on her husband's grave the words:

He has gone to the only place
Where his own works are excelled.

Here Lyes

HENRY PURCELL Esq.

Who left this Life

And is gone to that Blessed Place

Where only his Harmony

can be exceeded...

Cricketers' graves often have bat, ball, bails and wicket carved upon them, though I have yet to see the one in Oxfordshire that is said to bear the word 'Howzat!'

Then there is another untraced one to Henry Hardwick 'who by a cricket ball was struck' and on his tombstone is written, 'Hardwick, hard ball, hard luck'.

Richard (R.G.) Barlow, the famous Lancashire cricketing all-rounder, scored nearly 8,000 runs in his career and captured 736 wickets. He played in Australia three times and was famously hymned in a poem by Francis Thompson: 'O my Hornby and my Barlow long ago.' On his grave in Layton Cemetery, Blackpool – showing a bat, and a ball smashing through a wicket – is the simple inscription: "Bowled at last".

As for Tom Richardson, a Surrey and England cricketer, buried in Richmond Cemetery, Grove Road, Richmond, Surrey, this is quoted in Hugh Meller, *London Cemeteries* (1981):

He bowled his best but was himself bowled by the best on July 2nd 1912.

Harold Rauch of Burnham, Buckinghamshire, once worked as a gardener in a cemetery in Vienna. He told BBC Radio *Quote...Unquote* (13 September 1999) that one of the deceased must have been of extraordinary faith, he says, because the tombstone read, '*Hier liegt bis auf Widerruf / Leonhard Franz Futterknecht*', which being translated is:

Here lies
Leonhard Franz Futterknecht
– until further notice.

From Lydford Church, Devon. Geoffrey N. Wright, *Discovering Epitaphs* (1972) has this extended version – as well as the information that the inscription is on the upper surface of a chest-tomb. *Benham's Book of Quotations* (1948) has an extract, but puts the name as 'George Roughfield'.

Here lies, in horizontal position,
the outside case of
GEORGE ROUTLEIGH, Watchmaker;
Whose abilities in that line
Were an honour to his profession.
Integrity was the Mainspring, and prudence the Regulator
Of all the actions of his life.
Humane, generous and liberal,
his Hand never stopped till he had relieved Distress.
So nicely regulated were all his motions,
that he never went wrong,
except when set a-going by people
who did not know his Key;
Even then he was easily set right again.
He had the art of disposing his time so well,
that his hours glided away
in one continual round of pleasure and delight,
until an unlucky minute put a period
to his existence.
He departed this life,
Nov. 14, 1802,
aged 57:
wound up, in hopes of being taken in hand
by his Maker;
and of being thoroughly cleaned, repaired,
and set a-going in the world to come.

A Collection of Epitaphs and Monumental Inscriptions (1806) has this. It is on the *gravestone of Stephen Rumbold, born February 1582, died 4 March 1687, aged 105. The stone is now to be found under a mat in the porch of the Church of St Bartholomew, Brightwell Baldwin, Oxfordshire. It looks as if it has been re-cut. The deceased's name continues to be remembered locally in 'Rumbold's Lane' and 'Rumbold's Copse' (possibly on the site of his house).

He liv'd
one hundred and five
Sanguine and Strong
An hundred to five
You do not live
so long.

This example of a popular epitaph for blacksmiths can be found on a *grave by the south side of St Michael and All Angels, Ledbury, Herefordshire. It appears on an upright slab bearing at the top the name of Russell's wife Marriot who predeceased him in 1823. The final couplet is no longer legible, as the stone has crumbled, but may be supplied from William Andrews, *Curious Epitaphs* (1899).

The rhyme has been attributed to a poet called 'Hayley' and the example, said to date from 1746 in the churchyard of St Bartholomew, Nettlebed, Oxfordshire, is one of the earliest. On the other hand, if the poet was William Hayley, he was only born in 1745.

Benham's Book of Quotations (1948) cites a version 'in Awre churchyard, Gloucestershire, in memory of John Shaw, blacksmith, of Blakeney, d. Dec 24, 1743.'

Of the three versions of the rhyme from Midlands churches quoted in the *Oxford Book of Local Verses*, each has only six lines. *A Collection of Epitaphs and Monumental Inscriptions* (1806) has an eight line version, to William Braithwaite (who died in 1757), from St Albans, Hertfordshire.

As recently as 1926, Jabez White, a blacksmith buried in Charlton Cemetery, London SE7, was commemorated with this short version:

My anvil's worn my forge decayed
My body in the dust is laid
My coal is burnt my iron's run
My last nail is in my work is done.

In memory
of...
THOMAS RUSSELL,
Blacksmith of this Town...
who Died 24th May 1838
Aged 46 Years.

My Sledge and Hammer lie reclined,
My Bellows too have lost their wind.
My Fires extinct, my Forge decayed
And in the dust my Vice is laid.
My Coal is spent, my Iron gone,
My Nails are drove, my work is done;
My Fire-dried Corpse lies here at rest,
And, Smoke-like, soars up to be bless'd.

Maurice Selbach's *tombstone in Streatham Park Cemetery, Rowan Road, London SW16, not only incorporates a small portrait of him but also a carving of his bicycle (with drop handlebars) and a signpost. Peter Soper of the Veteran-Cycle Club wrote (2000): 'He was a fine racing cyclist who represented Great Britain in international championships. He later manufactured top-class bicycles, until he was killed in a road accident. His name was known to millions, which may explain the brevity of the inscription.'

R.I.P.

HE DIED
AS HE LIVED
A CYCLIST.

IN LOVING MEMORY OF
MY DEAR HUSBAND

MAURICE C. SELBACH
WHO WAS KILLED WHILST CYCLING
SEPTEMBER 26. 1935. AGED 46.
"UNTIL WE MEET AGAIN."

MY DEAR HUSBAND
JOHN RIGBY,
WHO DEPARTED THIS LIFE
OCT 4TH 1915 AGED 72 YEARS.
"AT REST".
ALSO FRANCES, WIFE OF THE ABOVE,
DIED APRIL 3RD 1928, AGED 85 YEARS
ALSO DORIS W. DAUGHTER OF
F & E RIGBY, DIED DEC. 24TH 1927,
AGED 2 YEARS & 3 MONTHS.
ALSO ELEANOR RIGBY
THE BELOVED WIFE OF THOMAS WOODS
AND GRANDDAUGHTER OF THE ABOVE
DIED 10TH OCT. 1939, AGED 44 YEARS
ASLEEP
ALSO FRANCES,
DAUGHTER OF THE ABOVE
DIED 2ND NOVEMBER 1940,
YEARS

Could this *grave have been the inspiration for the name 'Eleanor Rigby' in the Lennon and McCartney song (1967) – one of the 'lonely people' who 'died in the church and was buried along with her name'?

Although the two Beatles do not appear to have been consciously aware of the name on the Rigby family grave at St Peter's Church, Church Road, Woolton, Liverpool, there is the not inconsiderable coincidence that they famously first met during a church fête at St Peter's in 1957.

The real Eleanor Rigby seems to have died quite young, however, with a husband and daughter, and not exactly a lonely person. Perhaps it was just her name that lodged in the Beatle mind.

... ALSO ELEANOR RIGBY

THE BELOVED WIFE OF THOMAS WOODS

AND GRANDDAUGHTER OF THE ABOVE

DIED 10TH OCT 1939 AGED 44 YEARS

ASLEEP

In the church at Markham, Norfolk, is an inscription that clearly demands annotation. Christopher was the product of an incestuous relationship between the said Alice and her father. He left home as young boy and returned as a young man. Christopher and Alice did not recognize each other, he took her as his mistress and subsequently married her. It is said that Alice later her identified her son, lover and husband by a mole on his body and realized what she had done. Christopher put this inscription on their joint memorial (Alice predeceased him).

Here Lies the body of
Christopher Burraway, who
departed this life 18 day of
October, 1730 aged 59 years
And their Lies Alice, who by her
life was my sister, my mistress,
my mother, and my wife. Died
February 12, 1729 aged 76 years.

Almost an *epitaph. It is to be found over the West Door, on the outside of Staunton Harold church, Leicestershire. Sir Robert Shirley (b.1629) incensed Oliver Cromwell by building such a magnificent church. Cromwell said that the man who could afford to build it could pay for a regiment. Shirley, a Royalist, declined and was sent to the Tower where he died at the age of twenty-seven. He is buried beneath the chancel of the church.

In the yeare 1653
when all thinges Sacred were
throughout the nation
Either demollisht or
profaned
Sir Robert Shirley,
Barronet
Founded this Church
whose singular praise it is
to have done the best
thinges in the worst times
And
hoped them in the most
callamitous.
The righteous shall be had
in everlasting remembrance.

Benjamin Franklin put this epitaph in a letter to Georgiana Shipley on the death of her pet squirrel, Mungo (26 September 1772). 'Skug' was an American dialect word for squirrel. Having produced a full-blown epitaph for Mungo, Franklin says how much better it is than this short one.

Note this, however; Christopher W. Tarry of Bishop's Stortford, Hertfordshire, sent me some epitaphs included in the July 1816 edition of *The New Monthly Magazine*. Passing on epitaphs in this way was a popular activity in the 19th century. Early issues of *Notes and Queries* are stuffed with them. Mr Tarry's eye was caught in particular by one from Waddington in Lancashire (formerly in Yorkshire). It is 'In memory of WILLIAM RICHARD PHELPS, late Boatswain of H.M.S. *Invincible*. He accompanied Lord Anson in his cruise round the world, and died April 21, 1789.' It goes on:

When I was like you,
For years not a few,
On the ocean I toil'd,
On the line I have broil'd
In Greenland I've shiver'd,
Now from hardship deliver'd,
Capsiz'd by old death,
I surrender'd my breath.
And now I lie snug
As a bug in a rug.

Mr Tarry (who was unable to locate the original on a visit to Waddington) wondered about that final phrase, never having seen it used on a gravestone before.

Note also, an even earlier use of the phrase. In the anonymous *Stratford Jubilee* (commemorating David Garrick's Shakespeare festival in 1769) we have:

> If she [a rich widow] has the mopus's [money]
> I'll have her, as snug as a bug in a rug.

I suspect it was probably an established expression even by the second half of the 18th century – if only because in 1706, Edward Ward in *The Wooden World Dissected* had the similar 'He sits as snug as a Bee in a Box' and in Thomas Heywood's play *A Woman Killed with Kindness* (1603), there is 'Let us sleep as snug as pigs in pease-straw.'

Here Skugg
Lies snug
As a bug
In a rug.

Fritz Spiegl, *A Small Book of Grave Humour* (1971) has this as a 'memorial' to the Mormon leader who died in 1877 leaving 17 wives (so no doubt his 'superb equipment' came in useful). 'This spot' would have been Whitingham, Vermont.

Clearly a joke epitaph, but presumably making use of a phrase that was used in some way about Brigham Young.

BRIGHAM YOUNG
BORN
ON THIS SPOT
1801
A MAN OF MUCH
COURAGE
AND SUPERB
EQUIPMENT.

In the city of Lichfield, Staffordshire, not far from the Cathedral and near what used to be the Public Library, is a small park. Standing in it, somewhat forlornly, is a statue to – of all people – the captain of the *Titanic*. As I understand it, Commander Smith had nothing to do with Lichfield at all. He was born some miles away in Hanley, Staffordshire, and the statue was wished upon this unlikely spot when his native town rejected it. However, when quite recently Stafford tried to get the statue back, Lichfield apparently refused.

Under the figure, bearded and in naval uniform, now a very green bronze, is the *tablet bearing these words. The statue was unveiled by Smith's daughter on 29 July 1914 in the presence of the usual 'distinguished dignitaries' and Lady Scott – not only the statue's sculptor, but the widow of Capt. Scott, who perished in that other great British disaster of 1912, the fatal (for him) expedition to the South Pole.

As for 'Be British': Smith reputedly said, 'Be British, boys, be British' to his crew some time in the hours between the *Titanic* hitting its iceberg and his going down with the ship. Michael Davie in his book on the disaster describes the evidence for this as 'flimsy', but obviously the legend was already established by 1914 when the statue was erected.

CAPT. OF R.M.S. TITANIC
COMMANDER

EDWARD JOHN SMITH R.D. R.N.R.
BORN JANUARY 27 1850 DIED APRIL 15 1912
BEQUEATHING TO HIS COUNTRYMEN
THE MEMORY & EXAMPLE OF A GREAT HEART
A BRAVE LIFE AND A HEROIC DEATH.
BE BRITISH.

'In South Ealing cemetery', according to a correspondent, but untraced.

In memory of Jane Emily Smith

Died 10 Apr. 1804, aged 74

'Believing, we rejoice to see the curse removed'.

Mary Ann South had lived in the Hertfordshire village of Ayot St Lawrence for seventy years, from 1825 to 1895. Bernard Shaw, when asked why he chose to live in the same village, would explain that if the biblical span of three score years and ten was considered short there, it had to be a good place to live. He himself managed to live to the age of 94.

His observation is recorded in Michael Holroyd, *Bernard Shaw Vol. II: The Pursuit of Power* (1989). Hesketh Pearson, *Bernard Shaw* (1942) has that the inscription was 'Jane Evesley. Born 1815 – Died 1895. Her time was short.'

Was Short.

'On a comic post card [of a gravestone] at Blackpool'
– Bryan Glover on BBC Radio *Quote...Unquote*
(9 February 1982).

Miss Emily Stamp, postmistress.

Returned opened.

*Epitaph in the English cemetery on the island of San Michele, Venice, which was first drawn to my attention by Margaret R. Jackson, Chipping Campden (1982), though it had already been transcribed (inaccurately) in James Morris, *Venice* (1960/1974).

IN LOVING MEMORY
OF
FRANK STANIER
OF
STAFFORDSHIRE
WHO LEFT US IN PEACE
FEB. 2ND. 1910

On the 'eminent barrister, Sir John Strange' – W. Fairley, *Ephitaphiana* (1875); 'on Mr Strange, a lawyer' – William Tegg, *Epitaphs, Witty, Grotesque, Elegant &c.* (1876). The only notable lawyer of this name mentioned in the *Dictionary of National Biography* is Sir John Strange (1696–1754), who was Master of the Rolls.

Compare what John Aubrey earlier recorded: 'Ben JO(H)NSON, riding through Surrey, found the Women weeping and wailing, lamenting the Death of a Lawyer, who lived there: He enquired why so great Grief for the Losse of a Lawyer? Oh, said they, we have the greatest Loss imaginable; he kept us all in Peace and Quietness, and was a most charitable good Man: Whereupon Ben made this Distich: "God works Wonders now and then, / Behold a Miracle, deny't who can, / Here lies a *Lawyer* and an *honest* man." 'Tis Pity that good Man's Name should not be remember'd.'

Here lies an honest lawyer, –

That is Strange.

This *grave is easily located near one of the paths leading to the West Door of Winchester Cathedral, and was recorded in *A Collection of Epitaphs and Monumental Inscriptions* (1806). The stone was 'again replaced by the Royal Hampshire Regiment 1966' and this is duly recorded on it.

Bill Wilson, the American co-founder of Alcoholics Anonymous, recalled seeing the inscription when in Europe as a soldier on his way to the First World War and called it an 'ominous warning – which I failed to heed'.

In Memory Of
THOMAS THETCHER
a Grenadier in the North Reg.
of Hants Milita, who died of a
violent Fever contracted by drinking
Small Beer when hot the 12th of May
1764, Aged 26 Years.

In grateful remembrance of whose universal
good will towards his Comrades, this Stone
is placed here at their expence as a small
testimony of their regard and concern.

Here sleeps in peace a Hampshire Grenadier
Who caught his death by drinking cold small Beer.
Soldiers be wise from his untimely fall
And when ye're hot drink Strong or none at all.

*This memorial being decay'd was restor'd
by the Officers of the Garrison A.D. 1781.*

An honest Soldier never is forgot
Whether he died by Musket or by Pot.

*The Stone was replaced by the North Hants
Militia when disembodied at Winchester
on 26th April 1802, in consequence of
the original Stone being destroyed.*

On the *memorial to Lord Thomson of Fleet (1894–1976) in St Paul's Cathedral crypt. Canadian-born Roy Thomson acquired extensive newspaper interests in Britain (Times Newspapers, in particular), and once memorably described commercial television as a 'licence to print money'. It is surely odd to call any man 'strange' on his memorial.

He gave a new direction to the British newspaper industry. A strange and adventurous man from nowhere, ennobled by the great virtues of courage and integrity and faithfulness.

On a *gravestone (restored) at Malmesbury, Wiltshire – an unlikely location, it might seem, for the event described, but the tiger had apparently escaped from a circus.

IN MEMORY OF
HANNAH TWYNNOY
Who died October 23rd 1703
Aged 33 Years.

In bloom of Life
She's snatchd from hence,
She had not room
To make defence;
For Tyger fierce
Took Life away.
And here she lies
In a bed of Clay,
Until the Resurrection Day.

William Andrews, *Curious Epitaphs* (1899), has it that Turner was a fish-hawker and is buried in Preston, Lancashire. His coinage of the word is said to have taken place at a meeting in the Preston Cock-pit in September 1833. 'Dicky' Turner evidently had a way of emphasizing words and, when it came to the need for 'entire' abstinence, he declared that 'nothing but the te-te-total will do'. 'That shall be the name!' declared a colleague, and so it was.

Beneath this stone are deposited the remains of RICHARD TURNER, author of the word *Teetotal* as applied to abstinence from all intoxicating liquors, who departed this life on the 27th day of October, 1846, aged 56 years.

'I am a great fan of literals and misprints but my late Uncle Tim's preoccupation with them was nigh-on obsessive. Visiting his grave a few years ago I noticed that a memorial plaque on a neighbouring tree was dedicated to the deceased ... [as here]. An eternal torment to poor Tim, I imagine' – Belinda Bauer, Cardiff in a letter to *The Independent* (2 March 2001).

In Lovnig Memory

'On the adjacent tombstones of a husband and wife, Myrtle Beach, South Carolina' – The Revd Jonathan Meyrick, Barbados (1982).

At rest with Jesus.

Asleep with Mary.

Said to be in the churchyard of Upton-upon-Severn, Worcestershire, and also displayed by a monumental mason in Great Bedwyn, Wiltshire – according to Geoffrey N. Wright, *Discovering Epitaphs* (1972). W. Fairley's *Epitaphiana* (1875) also has a version. Yet another has the deceased's name as 'McGill'.

Samuel Klinger, *Graveyard Laughter* (1979) has this from Bideford, Devon:

Here lies the Landlord of 'The Lion'
His hopes removed to lands of Sion.
His wife resigned to Heaven's will,
Will carry on the business still.

(Two years later)

Here lies the Landlord's loving wife,
Her soul removed from lands of strife.
She's gone aloft her spouse to tell
The Inn he left her turned out well.

Beneath this stone in hopes of Zion,
Doth lie the landlord of the Lion,
His son keeps on the business still,
Resigned upon the heavenly will.

Cited as 'very epigrammatic and ironical' (but not identified) in Armstrong's *Norfolk Diary*, an account of a parish priest's life in East Dereham. On 6 July 1853, Armstrong commented gratefully that, in his own, there was 'a paucity of those singular and joking epitaphs which disgrace many English churchyards'.

**Be thou what you think
I ought to have been.**

A suggested epitaph on a waiter, credited to the poet David McCord, American poet and university fundraiser (1897–1997), in 'Remainders' from *Bay Window Ballads* (1935).

George S. Kaufman, American playwright (1889–1961) is also credited with the line 'God finally caught his eye' in Scott Meredith, *George S. Kaufman and the Algonquin Round Table* (1974).

By and by
God caught his eye.

'Suffolk churchyard, on child who died at eighteen months'
– Philip Reder, *Epitaphs* (1969).

Came in,
Walked about,
Didn't like it,
Walked out.

'In a small churchyard on the Great Orme, Llandudno'
– Dorothy Dunn, North Gosforth (1982).

Don't weep for me now

Don't weep for me ever

I'm going to do nothing

For ever and ever.

Quoted by Michael Rosen on BBC Radio *Quote...Unquote* (8 March 1994), from Easingwold in North Yorkshire:

She lived with her husband
of fifty years and died in the
confident hope of a better life.

This well-known rhyming epitaph appeared in Revd John Booth, *Metrical Epitaphs Ancient and Modern* (1868). G.W.E. Russell, *Collections and Recollections* (1898) commented sniffily, 'With professedly comic epitaphs – the *crambe repetita* of "Cheltenham Waters" ... I do not purpose to insult the intelligence of my readers.' David Mackae, *A Pennyworth of Queer Epitaphs* (?1910) said it came from Droitwich, dated 1701. Peter Haining, *Graveyard Wit* (1973) has it in St Giles's Church, Cheltenham.

Here lie I and my three daughters,

All from drinking the Cheltenham waters.

While if we had kept to the Epsom salts,

We should not now be in these here vaults.

Revd John Booth, *Metrical Epitaphs Ancient and Modern* (1868) has this as 'Here I lie at the chancel door...'; William Tegg, *Epitaphs, Witty, Grotesque, Elegant &c.* (1876) has it in Dawlish churchyard and at Kingsbridge church, Devon; W.H. Beable, *Epitaphs: Graveyard Humour & Eulogy* (1925) has it as being 'outside the Priest's Door, Kingsbridge Church, Devon ... in memory of Robert Phillip, commonly called Bone (due to he being the chief parish gravedigger) died 1795'.

Here lie I by the churchyard door.
Here lie I because I'm poor.
The farther in, the more you pay,
But here lie I as warm as they.

Sometimes referred to as 'The Maid-of-all-Works' Epitaph' or 'The Tired Woman's Epitaph', this has two possible sources. As 'an epitaph for Catherine Alsopp, a Sheffield washerwoman, who hanged herself, 7 August 1905', it was composed by herself and included in E. Jameson, *1000 Curiosities of Britain* (1937). But a letter in *The Spectator* (2 December 1922) from a correspondent at the British Museum states that the inscription was once to be found in Bushey churchyard. A copy of the text was made before 1860, but the actual stone had been destroyed by 1916.

Aubrey Stewart, *English Epigrams and Epitaphs* (1897) has it as 'quoted by James Payn in the *Cornhill Magazine*'. It was also discussed in *Notes and Queries* for March 1889 and *Longman's Magazine* for January 1884. *Cassell's Book of Quotations* (1907) states that it had been quoted 'before 1850'.

Here lies a poor woman who always was tired,

For she lived in a place where help wasn't hired,

Her last words on earth were,

'Dear friends, I am going,

Where washing ain't done nor cooking nor sewing,

And everything there is exact to my wishes,

For there they don't eat, there's no washing of dishes,

I'll be where loud anthems will always be ringing

(But having no voice, I'll be out of the singing).

Don't mourn for me now, don't grieve for me never,

For I'm going to do nothing for ever and ever'.

'In Freetown cemetery, West Africa' – F. Walter, London W6 (1982).

Recalling his military service in the late 1940s, Robert Robinson writes of a visit to Lagos in *Skip All That* (1997): 'Dr Azikiwe's newspaper, the *West African Pilot* ... [had] an obituary of an English bishop: this is the conventional lapidary thing, except for the last paragraph. It reads "It is not generally known that for the last thirteen years of his life the Bishop was a martyr to gonorrhoea".'

Here lie the remains of
His Grace the Bishop
of Sierra Leone who for
the last twenty years of
his life was a martyr to
gonorrhoea.

'Seen in a churchyard on Helston Riverside' – Mrs E. Brown, Thorpe Bay, Essex (1982). In 1993, John Oates of Wells sent me this fuller version from Mylor Bridge churchyard, also in Cornwall. 'In memory of Joseph Crapp shipwright who died 20th November, 1770 aged 43 years. Alas friend Joseph His End was Allmost Sudden As Thou [gh] the Mandate came Express from heaven, his foot it slip and he did fall he cries and that was all.' Perhaps they are one and the same inscription?

His end was all most sudden

As though the mandate came

express from Heaven

His foot it slipt and he did fall

'Help, help' he cried and that was all.

'For a child aged three weeks, Cheltenham Churchyard'
(17th century) – Bartlett's *Familiar Quotations* (1968):

It is so soon that

I wonder what

**I am done for,
I was begun for.**

'On a gravestone in Weston-super-Mare ... of course the joke only becomes clear when you realize that the words were originally spoken about an ass' – letter from the Revd S.G.N. Brindley, Sheffield (1981). Joke or not, it is quite a common text on gravestones.

The Lord hath

need of him.
Mark XI.3.

The poet John Clare (1793–1864) spent the last 27 years of his life in Northampton Lunatic Asylum. Accordingly, for a while, visitors to his grave in St Botolph's churchyard, Helpston, Cambridgeshire, might have marvelled at the appropriateness of the epitaph on it:

A POET IS BORN NOT MAD

Alas, when the old grave was cleaned up, it was found to read, rather:

A POET IS BORN NOT MADE.

Which brings us to the epitaph opposite. It is said to appear on the bottom of a Tasmanian tombstone. The 'e' is on the back, the stonemason not having left himself enough room to carve it on the front. Is there a source for this much-told joke? It is also told of a Presbyterian churchyard in the US in Charles L. Wallis, *Stories in Stone*: *A Book of American Epitaphs* (before 1969).

LORD SHE IS THIN

'From Kew, if I remember rightly, which might be about 1850 ... About half the tombstone is covered with a long panegyric on his dead wife by a bereaved husband. At the bottom of the stone is a later inscription which reads "Now he's gone too" ... Since the decay of the belief in personal immortality, death has never seemed funny, and it will be a long time before it does so again. Hence the disappearance of the facetious epitaph, once a common feature of country churchyards' – George Orwell in *Tribune* (14 February 1947).

NOW HE'S GONE TOO.

'On a gravestone at the Parish Church of Church Stretton, Salop' – J. Turner, Canterbury (1982). It is on the grave of Ann Cook, died 1814.

On Thursday she was born,
On Thursday made a bride,
On Thursday her leg was broke,
And on Thursday she died.

'From Kersey, Suffolk' – Mrs B.M. Moss, Bourne, Lincolnshire (1982). Samuel Klinger (1979) has a similar verse from 'West Down, Devonshire, 1797' as well as from Guildford, Surrey. Compare:

Stranger, pass by and waste no time
On bad biography and careless rhyme.
For what I am, this humble dust discloses;
And what I was is no affair of yourses

– described as a 'Suffolk epitaph, 1870' in *The Week-End Book* (1955).

Reader, pass on nor waste thy time

On bad biography or bitter rhyme

For what I am my humble dust enclose

And what I was is no affair of yours.

The perfect epitaph on John Stone, a clerk, found in Hull by Joan Bakewell and John Drummond for their book *A Fine and Private Place* (1977):

Excellent,

in his way.

'Put by a loving wife in memory of her husband, Hindhead, Surrey' – Patricia Spencer, Edgware, London, (1981). Quoted without source in Jessica Mitford, *The American Way of Death*, Chap. 4 (1963):

Rest in Peace
Until we meet again.

'An In Memoriam notice from the Calcutta *Statesman* in the 1930s' – K.W. Bevan (1982). 'Safe in the Arms of Jesus' is the title of a Moody and Sankey type chorus, words by F.J. Crosby. J.B. Morrell, *The Biography of the Common Man of the City of York* (1948) cited a newspaper 'In Memoriam' notice that 'might have been expressed better':

In loving memory of our grandson Peter
Safe in the arms of Jesus
From Grandma, Aunties and Uncles.

Safe in the arms of Jesus.
(inserted by her loving husband).

'From the famous tombstone of Plymouth, Tobago, dating from 1783. Copied from a leaflet issued by the Trinidad and Tobago Tourist Board, "which inscription baffles interpretation"' – C. Millett, Baltimore, Maryland (1982):

She was a Mother
without knowing it,
And a Wife,
without letting her
Husband know it,
Except by her kind
indulgences to him.

'Traditional, from Ireland', quoted on BBC Radio *Quote... Unquote* (2 March 1982):

Wherever you be
Let your wind go free.
For it was keeping it in
That was the death of me.

Puns on the 'Here lies ... ' theme take two forms. One may be intended on the grave of the poet and writer Laurie Lee (1914–97) at Slad in Gloucestershire. His chosen wording:

> He lies in the
> valley he loved.

Those who consider that Lee was an incorrigible liar have suggested that he deliberately wanted the double meaning of 'lies'.

The second type occurs, for example, in this epitaph on Sir John Vanbrugh (1664–1726), the dramatist and architect. It was written by Dr Abel Evans (1679–1737) thinking of Blenheim Palace – though it has also been ascribed to the architect, Nicholas Hawksmoor. The version here is the one in Booth, *Metrical Epitaphs Ancient and Modern* (1868). *A Collection of Epitaphs and Monumental Inscriptions* (1806) has:

> Lie light upon him earth! tho' he
> Laid many a heavy load on thee.

Compare, on the statesman Henry Pelham:

> Lie heavy on him, land, for he
> Laid many a heavy tax on thee.

Vanbrugh is buried in the North Aisle of St Stephen's Church, Walbrook, City of London. His wife was later buried within this family vault but no sign of any such epitaph is apparent. It was presumably never more than a suggested epitaph.

Cassell's Book of Quotations (1907) compares the Latin, '*Sit tibi terra gravis!*' ('May the earth be heavy upon thee'), which contrasts with '*Sit tibi terra levis!*' – ('Let the earth lie light upon you', sometimes abbreviated to 'S.T.T.L.').

Under this stone, Reader, survey

Dead Sir John Vanbrugh's house of clay.

Lie heavy on him, Earth! for he

Laid many heavy loads on thee!

'Tablet in the church of Ashover, Derbyshire' – William Andrews, *Curious Epitaphs* (1899):

To the Memory of

DAVID WALL

whose superior performance on the

bassoon endeared him to an

extensive musical acquaintance.

His social life closed on the

4th Dec., 1796, in his 57th year.

On a tombstone in the Presidio area of San Francisco.
Discovered on a postcard by Sir David Hunt during the
Second World War:

Here lies the body of
George Warburton
late of Guildford, England,

who died 23 October 1850
by the explosion of his own pistol.
It was one of the modern sort
but an old-fashioned breech-loader
with the barrel bound in brass wire.
And of such is the
kingdom of Heaven.

Translation of a Latin inscription to be found in the Old Cloisters at Winchester College – John Julius Norwich, *More Christmas Crackers* (1990):

Beneath this Marble is Buried
Tho. Welsted
Who was Struck Down by the
Throwing of a Stone.
He was First in this School
And we Hope is not Last in Heaven
Whither he went
Instead of to Oxford.
January 13, 1676
Aged 18.

An epitaph by the American poet John Greenleaf Whittier (1807–92) on his cat Bathsheba:

To whom none ever said scat,
No worthier cat
Ever sat on a mat
Or caught a rat:
Requies—cat.

From Mrs E.M. Hollingworth, Huddersfield (1981):

Here lies the body of Emily White,

She signalled left, and then turned right.

I first heard this final one given as an 'epitaph on a hypo-chondriac'. The 'sick' version was quoted by the American writer Paul Theroux on BBC Radio *Quote...Unquote* (22 December 1981), though he did not say where he had got it from. Subsequently, I may have heard that it was supposed to have originated, rather vaguely, in 'the southern US'.

The only report I received that anything like the epitaph had appeared anywhere at all in the US, came when I was told that it was carved on the Hermine [Hermione?] E. and Thomas P. Connelly gravestone in the Forest Hill Cemetery in East Derry, New Hampshire. There is as yet no confirmation of this.

Further research turned up two other mentions of this 'sick' version: in Robert Ramsay and Randall Toye's *The Goodbye Book*, published by Van Nostrand Reinhold (1979). Ramsay and Toye were pretty careful about giving sources for their material so it is disappointing that their only note on 'I told you I was sick' reads 'In a Georgia cemetery.' It turned up also in Ed Morrow's *The Grim Reaper's Book of Days: A Cautionary Record of Famous, Infamous and Unconventional Exits*, a Citadel Press Book, published by Carol Publishing Group (1992). Under June 18, 1979, it has: 'Key West, Florida. B.P. Roberts died at age 50. His tombstone reads: "I TOLD YOU I WAS SICK".'

In 2004, Robert Deis of Cudjoe Key, Florida, confirmed that a large white crypt in the Key West Cemetery does indeed have a *tablet that states:

Continued from page 282

He added that, according to local legend, Pearl Roberts was, in fact, a waitress who people viewed as a laughable hypochondriac, but who apparently had the last laugh.

So at least we know the epitaph had some scattered popularity by 1979 and, it would seem, in more than one place within the US. Indeed, it was probably an American fad in origin but the popularity of the joke spread far and wide and various other uses have been reported – for example, 'SEE, I TOLD YOU I WAS SICK', on the Waine family *grave at Boston (this apparently dates from 1990). I have no idea where it really originated or when. In 2004, Anne Tayler wrote to me: 'In the 1960s, I shared an office with a man called Frank Granville Barker [the music critic] and he told this story, with the inscription being: "I told you I wasn't feeling very well", which I think is funnier.' So does this story point to a British origin?

Moves to put the joke on graves in the British Isles do not seem to have been made until well after the American ones. In January 1994, it was reported that the dying wish of Keith Woodward, a barber of Shrivenham, Wiltshire, had been to have a tombstone bearing his favourite joke – 'I told them I was ill' – written on it. However, when he was buried beneath the inscription in a village cemetery, parish councillors objected that the words were unacceptable and ordered the message to be removed.

Continued from page 285

Then, in 2002, when Spike Milligan died, it was reported that he also wanted 'I told you I was *ill*' to be his epitaph. Indeed, *I Told You I Was Ill* was the title of a memorial tribute to the Irish-born comedian and humorous writer at Guildhall, London (15 September 2002). At first, possibly owing to family hesitation and clerical doubts, it looked as though the words would not be appearing over his grave in St Thomas's churchyard, Winchelsea, East Sussex. Whatever the reason for the delay, it should be obvious from the foregoing that Milligan did not originate the joke.

By 2004, however, Milligan was duly resting under a *gravestone in the shape of a Celtic cross. Beginning with the English words, 'Love, light, peace', the inscription goes on to describe him as, 'Writer ◆ Artist ◆ Musician ◆ Humanitarian ◆ Comedian'.

And then comes his epitaph, discreetly put in Irish:

Duirt me leat go raibh me breoite

This does indeed mean, 'I told you I was Ill' or 'I told you I was sick' – translate it how you will.

PICTURE CREDITS